Faithfully adhering to the biblical narrative, Tim Roehl has written sensitive and compelling portrayals of the characters of the Christmas story. As they react to the coming of the Christ Child into their world, they come alive in our hearts and minds, and we ourselves are drawn closer to Him through them. . . .

PETER MARSHALL JR.
Peter Marshall Ministries

Christmas may seem to us like a story from a faraway land with exotic wisemen and kings who have little to do with our everyday lives. But author Tim Roehl pictures for us the people of Christmas as real people, in real places, with the same real fears and longings you and I have. *Christmas Hearts* helps us to see the heart of Christmas—a God who came in the flesh and moved into the neighborhood. I warmly recommend it.

LEIGHTON FORD
Leighton Ford Ministries
Charlotte, NC

Christmas Hearts is splendid and delightful reading. It will minister to hosts of people, not only during the Christmas season but year round. Your heart will be warmed as you see through the eyes of His contemporaries the glorious Incarnation of the Babe of Bethlehem.

TED ENGSTROM
President Emeritus, World Vision

Christmas Hearts

Images of Immanuel Through the Eyes
of Those Who Saw Him First

TIM ROEHL

Illustrations by
Keith Mueller

PROMISE
PRESS

An Imprint of Barbour Publishing

© 1998 by Tim Roehl

Original art by Keith Mueller, Copyright 1998 by Keith Mueller. All rights reserved.

ISBN 1-57748-377-4

Published by Promise Press, an imprint of Barbour Publishing, Inc., P.O. Box 719, Uhrichsville, Ohio 44683
http://www.barbourbooks.com

 Member of the
Evangelical Christian
Publishers Association

Printed in the United States of America.

Dedication

To my mom. . .
who first saw promise in my words
and spoke into my heart a vision to write.

Table of Contents

Some Words from the Author

For as long as I can remember, I've been going to church. Jesus was part of my culture, viewed through stained glass windows and Sunday school "pix" comics. When I was sixteen, however, I met Jesus—the real Jesus—as my Savior.

Shortly after that, for a speech competition, my high school English teacher suggested that I review some sermon material from Peter Marshall, a pastor and former chaplain of the U.S. Senate. Sermon stuff for speech? At first I was not interested, until I began to read Peter Marshall's messages. With "sanctified imagination" he retold biblical accounts in such a vivid way that I felt like I was right there in the story. Most importantly, Peter showed me a Jesus that strode off the pages of the Bible and right into my heart. Peter helped me truly "see" Jesus. This was the Jesus I wanted to know! And Peter ignited in me a passion to help others know Him, too.

The stories in *Christmas Hearts* are an overflow of that passion. I want you to "see" the real Jesus of the Bible.

It is my prayer that you'll say, like I did, "That's the Jesus I want to know, too."

It's Never Too Late

He stood in the doorway of his home, looking out across the hills of Judea into the setting sun. Sundown always brought a streaky mixture of oranges and reds, blending into deeper shades of purple and gray. He was always amazed at the way the shadows could reshape those hills a thousand different ways.

It's getting to be sundown for me, too, he thought. Wrinkles lined the skin around his eyes and his beard was threaded with gray. In spite of the marks of accumulated years, however, his eyes still sparkled like those of a man whose heart was much younger.

He felt a hand on his shoulder and turned to see the face of his beloved wife, Elizabeth. Her eyes, too, had a youthful twinkle that made the wrinkles on her face a mark of gentle grace rather than advancing age.

"Thinking again, my husband?" she asked softly. "You've been doing a lot of that lately."

For a moment he was silent, a faraway look in his eyes that focused beyond the hills to some unrealized dream. Then he spoke quietly, the words flowing from deep within his heart.

"I've been thinking about our lives, Elizabeth. I've been thinking about our people. Here in the later years of our ministry, we serve out in the hills. I know we could be serving in a bigger city with more people, but they need us out here. All these years all I've wanted to do was serve God the very best way I knew how. All I've wanted was to teach His people from His Word and pass on our heritage of faith to our children. God knows my heart. . .He knows we've tried to serve Him honestly. We've been faithful to Him. . . ."

He turned to his wife of many years, putting his hands on the shoulders of the one who had ministered so faithfully at his side. Looking into her face, his own eyes showed deep sadness and pain.

"And yet we have no children, no son to carry on our name, no son to pass on our love for the Lord. What have we done that we bear this reproach of barrenness?"

Without waiting for an answer, he looked out over the hills again and said, "And I've been thinking about our people. For over four hundred years now God has been silent. No word from a prophet or an angel. No miraculous sign of His presence. We live under the tyranny of the Romans. Slaves to them. . .and even worse, slaves to sin. When will God send us the Messiah? When will He set His people free in their hearts and free in their land?"

His eyes glowed with a deep passion, and for a moment he seemed to carry not only his own private pain but the weight of his whole nation as well.

"My name is Zechariah—'the Lord remembers.' But will He remember me? It seems to be too late for our dreams to ever come true."

Then his tense muscles relaxed, and he smiled. "Dear wife, how can you put up with the words of an old man like me?"

She gazed up at him with a look of admiration for her man, this husband of hers, this faithful priest of God. Her quiet smile was a better answer than any words she could say.

He looked at her lovingly in return. Taking her hand, he said, "Tomorrow our division of priests goes to the Temple in Jerusalem to serve before the Lord. Perhaps this time He will show me He has heard our prayers and give us cause to rejoice yet in our old age."

There were twenty-four divisions of priests in Israel. Twice each year a division was required to serve in the Temple in Jerusalem. There they would perform the sacred duties of offering up sacrifices before the Lord for the sins of the people. Twice each day a priest, chosen by lot, would have the special privilege of going into the Holy Place to burn incense, signifying the prayers of God's people. Because there were so many priests, a priest could only make the incense offering once in his entire lifetime, and some never got the honored privilege. Standing before God for an entire nation was no small responsibility.

During this week of ministry, Zechariah's name was chosen for him to go into the Holy Place to offer incense. Every priest dreamed of this opportunity. Zechariah breathed a prayer of gratitude to the Lord for his long hoped-for privilege to minister before the altar of incense.

The morning sun was warming Jerusalem. On this Sabbath, the courts of the Temple were filling with worshippers. They entered through the gate of the Temple called Beautiful and into the courtyards. Each area allowed people to come closer to God, although each court represented a kind of spiritual segregation. The Outer Court of the Gentiles allowed people of non-Jewish descent to approach God. . .to a point. The Women's Court, one step "closer" to God, allowed them to worship there. Next came the Court of Men. It was for Jewish males who were living according to the Law and it allowed them closer than the Gentiles and women. The next court, the Inner Court, was reserved especially for priests to minister to God on behalf of the people. Finally, the Innermost Place. . .the most sacred of all. The Holy of Holies contained the Ark of the Covenant. . .and, they believed, the Presence of their Holy God.

Only the High Priest could enter the Holy of Holies, and then only once a year. He would enter the Holiest Place and pour blood on the Mercy Seat of the Ark. It was there that forgiveness was purchased by blood for the nation, allowing a Holy God to be reconciled with very unholy people. For every faithful priest of God, the greatest possible joy came in seeing the peace of God come to a pardoned heart. Zechariah's passion had always been to know God and as God's man help people return to a right relationship with Him. That was what made this opportunity to offer prayer for his people such a privilege.

Zechariah, heart beating fast and eyes bright, walked slowly into the Inner Court. The Holy Place. Here no sunlight ever reached. Inside was the table of the shewbread to the left, the sacred candlestand on the right, and the altar of incense right in front of the veil that hid the Holy of Holies. The entire room was overlaid with gold, and as Zechariah entered, now the lone representative of Israel before God, he was awed by the golden luster cast by the light of the candles.

This was indeed a sacred place.

He approached the altar, casting incense on the burning coals. The air filled with a fragrant perfume that wafted to the outer courts. Zechariah breathed deeply the wonderful fragrance, savoring the moment. Then he stepped back and offered his prayer, both for himself and for his people. Quietly he poured his heart out to God, his whole being hungering for God to move among His people again.

Suddenly, to the right of the altar an angel appeared. Zechariah had never seen an angel, nor did he know what one looked like, but the air was charged with divine electricity and throbbed with the power of holiness. There was no mistake—this was a messenger from God!

Involuntarily, Zechariah took a step back, his eyes huge. For four hundred years there had been no supernatural revelation from God, and now, here standing before him, was an angel from heaven itself. What had he done? Had he offered an unacceptable prayer? Was God here to tell him of His judgment coming to the nation? Was he going to die? It had often been said that no mortal could be in the presence of a divine being and stay alive.

The angel spoke, his voice deep but gentle.

"Do not be afraid, Zechariah. Your prayer has been heard. Your wife, Elizabeth, will bear you a son, and you are to give him the name John. He will be a joy and delight to you, and many will rejoice because of his birth, for he will be great in the sight of the Lord. He is never to take wine or other fermented drink, for he will be filled with the Holy Spirit even from birth. Many of the people of Israel will he bring back to the Lord their God. And he will go on before the Lord, in the spirit and power of Elijah, to turn the hearts of the fathers to their children and the disobedient to the wisdom and attitude of the righteous—to make ready a people prepared for the Lord."

"A son. . ." The words seemed too good to be true. For a moment Zechariah's heart sought to grasp and hold onto the promise of the Lord, spoken through the angel. . .but then he lost his grip as he realized that he and his wife were both barren and old. If only, if only he could have a sign, then he could believe. Slowly, his voice barely above a whisper, he said, "How can I be sure of this? I am an old man and my wife is well along in years. Perhaps a sign. . . ?"

The angel spoke again, his deep voice now taking a firmer tone. "I am Gabriel, God's Mighty One. I stand in the presence of God, and I have been sent to speak to you and tell you this good news. And now, because you could not take God at His Word, you shall have your sign. You will be silent and unable to speak until the day this happens, because you did not believe my words, which will come true at their proper time."

With that, the angel vanished. Zechariah tried to ask him to wait, but he found he was unable to speak.

When he stumbled out of the Holy Place back among the people, they looked at him in amazement as he tried to signal with his hands what had happened. Even with words, how do you tell people that for the first time in four hundred years, God had spoken to His people again? How do you help people understand that their religion was about to take on the element of the supernatural instead of just form and ritual?

Faithful man that he was, Zechariah completed his week of service in silence and returned home with his wife. Only a few weeks later after they had returned home, she met him at the door with the incredible news: She was going to have a baby! They danced with joy around their small home at the incredible prospect—two senior citizens needed to add a nursery to their home! The miracle had begun!

For nine months Zechariah and Elizabeth waited, he in silence, she humming happy songs as she made baby clothes and chatted cheerfully with the neighbor ladies about the joys of motherhood. For several months their young relative Mary from Nazareth lived with them. The news she brought was even more miraculous than theirs. Watching his Elizabeth spontaneously prophesy as their son leapt in her womb when Mary arrived was an awe-inspiring event. Listening to his Elizabeth tenderly minister to Mary, the mother of the Messiah, was a joy. Here under his roof were the two women who carried in their wombs the one who would prepare the way and the One who would pardon humanity. Often he found himself silently watching and listening in wonder.

His silence was not passive, however. In his enforced quietness, he listened to the Spirit of God as never before in his life, and God revealed His great plan of redeeming a world of fallen people. His son would prepare the way for the long-awaited Messiah! John would have the kind of ministry not seen since Elijah, one of fiery preaching and fearless confrontation with sin, calling people to repent and turn to God. His son. . .preparing the way for people to meet the Lord, guiding their feet into the path of peace.

God's heart-desire was for people everywhere—men, women, Jews, Gentiles, rich, poor—to know Him with no barriers or segregation. The Temple was the place where God resided, but it segregated people by gender and class. God's plan, full of wonder to a Jewish priest, was to unite all humanity in the person of His Messiah, regardless of education, ethnic group, or economic standing. He would come to live, not in a building, but in believing hearts! His Holy Place would be in humble hearts!

The thought stretched Zechariah's perspective, but as he pondered God's Word, he knew it to be true. Salvation would come through the nation of Israel, but it would be available to the whole world! His son. . .clearing the way for people to see Almighty God, the Redeemer Himself! The Messiah. . .the One who would be like a Light in the darkness, the sunrise in the night of humanity's depravity. He would illuminate the way to God so all could come in simple faith. He would set people free to truly know God. He would take down all the barriers between God and humanity, between races, between genders, between classes, between nations. In Him all people would find their identity, their security, and their eternity. The months of waiting with Elizabeth gave birth to revelations full of wonder in Zechariah's own heart. He longed to tell others the incredible truths God was revealing to him, but first would have to come the birth of his own son. Then he could verbalize the overflow of his heart.

Finally the wonderful day came. His Elizabeth had never looked so beautiful, even in the midst of the pains of childbirth. . .and then their son arrived! Laughter rang in Zechariah's house as the relatives and friends passed around the baby boy for all to see. When they placed him in Zechariah's arms, tears of joy ran down the creases of his cheeks.

Eight days later the day of naming the child came. The house was crowded with relatives and friends, each with a different opinion. "His name should be Zechariah, after his father, don't you think?" suggested one. Heads nodded in agreement, expecting Zechariah's and Elizabeth's assent.

"No. . .his name is John," said Elizabeth. When dozens of pairs of eyes turned to look quizzically at him, Zechariah motioned for a clay tablet.

He inscribed in the clay the words that confirmed his baby's name. Suddenly his tongue tingled, and Zechariah spoke. "His name is John." He was speaking! Eyes large with wonder, he looked at his beloved Elizabeth. "His name is John. . .God's gracious gift." Elizabeth nodded, tears of joy shining on her cheeks. His tongue was free to be heard again! The time of silence was over. The sign God reluctantly gave him months earlier was fulfilled at last.

This time the words out of his mouth were an overflow of praise to God. His anointed words are now known as the Benedictus. His was the last prophecy of the old covenant and the first of the new covenant. The old man who thought God had forgotten him saw his prayers answered beyond his greatest expectations.

Rocking his baby in his arms, the realization of all God would do through his son overwhelmed his heart. Truly God had remembered him! Yes, his name was indeed Zechariah!

Yes, he thought, *it's never too late for God.*

Made for a Miracle

*S*he walked along the path toward home, a water jar balanced on her head. Even though the weight of the clay jar full of water was quite heavy for a young woman scarcely into her teen years, she felt as if she was walking on air. Her heart was singing, and the earth, sky, and birds seemed to sing with her.

Mary was in love.

More than that, she was betrothed to be married to the handsome carpenter Joseph. So binding was the betrothal that if Joseph should die before their marriage, she would be legally his widow. Their covenant to be married could not be broken without going through a divorce. They were married in the legal though not the physical sense.

Soon. . .soon! would come the wedding feast. Joseph would arrive with his kinfolk up the path to her home, as was the custom in every wedding. Knocking joyfully on the door, he would call for his bride. Their rabbi would bless them and lead them through the joining ceremony. After much celebration, eating, and well wishing, the newly married couple would enter the bridal chamber. Then they could be fully married.

Married! Her Joseph was not a rich man, but there was about him the priceless quality of a sturdy, righteous character. He was a solid, yet tender man, and although he was a carpenter, the royal blood of the line of David flowed through his veins, as it did in hers. He was also a student of the Scriptures, with an awe for God unfortunately uncommon in young men. Just past his twentieth year, in their day he was considered almost old to be getting married, for life was hard in the hills of Israel. Since life expectancy was not long, it was both normal and necessary to begin families early.

Yet he had waited for Mary to mature, for he loved Mary deeply. They carried in their hearts the precious knowledge that they were both pure. They kept themselves clean and innocent, awaiting the time when they could enjoy God's special gift to a husband and wife with His blessing and approval. Oh, there had been opportunities to sin sexually, but they both knew that waiting was far better than a stolen moment that could be regretted for a lifetime.

Somehow, although she couldn't really understand it, Mary carried a deep sense of God's hand on her life. She was made for a special purpose. Because of that heart-sense, she refused to make a shambles of God's purpose even when her emotions urged her body to do what came naturally. The waiting would be worth it. Her decision to stay pure was far more important than she could have ever dared to dream.

Lost in her thoughts of joyful anticipation, she looked up, a bit surprised to find that she was home. "Dreaming again," she said, smiling to herself.

Her mother teasingly accused her of doing that a lot lately. But. . .she was in love, and a heart overcrowded by love had a tendency to lose sight of other things. Just a few more short months, and she would be the wife of Joseph!

Entering the house, she saw her mother Hannah preparing the evening meal. As the oldest of the children, Mary's responsibilities were growing. She was even more conscious she needed to learn from her mother the important things of running a household. Soon she would be responsible for her own.

Her father Joachim's cheery voice shouted a greeting from a distance as he returned from the fields after a long day of work. Mary followed as the rest of the children ran out to meet him, and he caught up the youngest, hoisting him on his shoulder while the rest walked beside.

As Joachim approached his home, Mary met him on the path and slipped her hand in his in welcome. When he looked at her, his eyes were soft with a father's love. Not long ago—it seemed like yesterday—she had been the one happily riding on his shoulder. Now, here she was a woman soon to be married. His heart felt a bittersweet pang at the thought of no longer having her under his roof. Yet with Joseph as a son-in-law, he would be welcoming a good man into his family.

Father and children chatted about the events of the day, and then gathered around the table to bless and eat their food. They were not a rich family, but one wealthy in love. Lamplight shone from their windows, like it did from hundreds of other homes in the hills of Galilee. Nothing special marked their home from any other. . .yet in Heaven, this home was to be the place of the greatest miracle in human history.

Later, as she often did, Mary climbed up by herself onto the flat roof of the house to sit and watch the stars. The younger children were in bed, so she could enjoy these few moments alone. Stars glittered like diamonds against the spring sky's black velvet.

And to think that God knows each star by name, she thought. Just last Sabbath, their rabbi had read the passage from one of the prophets. She watched the stars in silent wonder, even more awed by the God who had created them. Could a God that powerful, that wise, that infinite, care about her? She was just one insignificant person in the middle of this vast universe. Did He really have a special plan for her, or was she just fooling herself?

A sudden radiance burst from behind her, unlike any light she had ever seen. Turning quickly to see where the light was coming from, she saw it radiated from a tall man standing a few feet from her. A glow surrounded him, but the light and the smile on his face was soft and warm. Strangely, she did not feel afraid. She sensed she was in the presence of an angel, though she had never seen one before.

He raised his hand in a familiar gesture of welcome. "Greetings, you who are highly favored! The Lord is with you." His voice was deep, his tone friendly, yet there was respect behind his words.

Respect. . .from an angel? The thought troubled and overwhelmed her. What could such a greeting mean? Why was she highly favored? What did he mean that God was with her?

The angel smiled and spoke again as if to answer her questions and ease her perplexity.

"Do not be afraid, Mary, for you have found favor with God. You will be with child and give birth to a Son, and you are to give Him the name JESUS. He will be great and will be called the Son of the Most High. The Lord God will give Him the throne of His father David, and He will reign over the house of Jacob forever. His Kingdom will never end."

His words were so unexpected, she did not know what to say. These were the words every woman of Israel longed to hear. . .and she was hearing them! The angel spoke with such certainty. . .

how was God going to make such a miracle possible? "How will this happen, since I am a virgin?" asked Mary. Her words carried not the tone of unbelief, but of trusting curiosity. She was not only hearing the angel's words, but also receiving them in simple faith into her heart.

"The Holy Spirit will come upon you, and the power of the Most High will overshadow you. So the Holy One to be born will be called the Son of God. Even Elizabeth your relative is going to have a child in her old age, and she who was said to be barren is in her sixth month. *For nothing is impossible with God.*"

For a moment time stood still. She soaked in the incredible significance of the angelic words. Every woman dreamed of being the mother of the Messiah. Every family prayed that their daughter might have the divine honor of bearing the Christ Child. Now God had appointed her! She was not worthy! She was no one special. . .yet God had chosen her! Mary's heart melted with wonder at the grace of God.

Then her thoughts sped to Joseph. How could she explain it to him? How could he understand this? It would seem that she had been unfaithful to him. What would her parents say? What of the wagging tongues in the village? The penalty for adultery—and that was surely what they would accuse her of—was death by stoning. Saying yes to God could cost her everything. . .her husband, her family, her reputation, her life.

Her mind weighed all these factors, and then her heart told her this was what God had designed her for all along. Nothing could compare with what God had planned for her. No price would be too much to pay.

In an act of complete yielding, she knelt and said, "I am the Lord's servant. May it be to me as you have said." She placed herself, like a servant girl, completely in God's hands, willing and ready to do whatever He wanted of her. Hers was the servant heart God had been looking for.

With a bright smile of acknowledgment, the angel nodded to her, and then was gone.

And so the greatest miracle of all began. Mary, the young, poor girl from the hills of Galilee, was overshadowed by the Glory of the Holy Spirit. God's Messiah was conceived in her womb. A virgin was pregnant with the Holy Child. God the Son clothed Himself with human flesh, wrapped in the heart and womb of Mary.

She would call Him Son.

The world would call Him Savior.

Our Dream, His Time

*L*ying on her bed, Elizabeth smiled up into the darkness. Beside her, her beloved Zechariah snored softly, a sound she had lovingly endured for many years. Her hand rested on her stomach as she felt the stirring of a young life inside her. Never before in all her years had she experienced the wonder of such a feeling, and she reveled in its pain and pleasure.

Elizabeth, the barren one, the aged one, was going to have a baby!

It had seemed like a dream months ago when her husband walked slowly out of the Holy Place with a look of awe on his face. His eyes sought out hers first, and with a look of wonder he had mouthed the words, "a son" to her. Later, when they were alone, he wrote and talked with his hands to relate to her the incredible story. This baby was such an intimate, personal gift to an old couple, that the name John, God's gracious gift, seemed totally appropriate to Elizabeth. Little did she know that the entire world would one day rise up and honor the name and ministry of John the Baptizer.

At first she was in a daze. She had all but given up hope of ever becoming a mother. Women in Israel who could not have children were scorned. They were considered cursed—under God's sentence of barrenness because of divine disapproval. Many a night Elizabeth had stared into the darkness, tears running down her cheeks and onto her pillow as she pleaded with God to show her what she had done wrong. Whatever it was, she would make it right! She had tried with all her heart to serve the Lord and her husband faithfully. Her heart convicted her of nothing, yet her womb was barren. Even Zechariah's gentle strength, reminding her of his love and God's love for her, did not remove the ache in her soul. Her name meant "consecrated to God," but the women of her town called her "the barren one."

"The barren one." Sometimes she would hear it whispered as she passed by a cluster of women talking, their children clinging to their skirts. Other times it only took a look, that certain kind of look women give each other that cuts like a knife. Women could be incredibly cruel, she knew, using only their tongue or a raised eyebrow as weapons.

Still, she had not acted in kind. She did not gossip about other people's problems or embarrassments, nor did she harbor bitterness toward them. Instead she continually lifted her hurt and her heart to the faithful God she served and loved. She did not understand why she could not conceive, but she trusted Him with what she did know. The Lord was just. Faithful. His love never failed. These were the realities she leaned on. There were times when she leaned hard. Meanwhile time continued until her childbearing years ran out like grains of sand in an hourglass. Still, she continued to trust the Lord, her heart full of trust even though her arms were empty.

Then came the silent, wonder-filled announcement of her husband! As it sank in, she had sat in her chair with hands clasped over her heart, looking to Heaven with her heart too full to speak. She knew, though, that the Lord could understand her unspoken thanks and praise perfectly. She had reached out, taking her husband's hand, her eyes shining like a new bride's as she said to him, "Yes, my beloved husband, we shall have a gift from God. . .a son. Our son."

After she became pregnant, she kept herself in seclusion for five months. Rarely did she go into town. She worked quietly at home, taking extra care of her aged body, now the home of two living souls. She would wait until it was very obvious that she was with child before she would let the women of the village see her. Then God's miracle would be revealed to all. They would see that it was God Himself who had taken away her reproach. Her devotion to Him had been rewarded. "The barren one" would now be described all over the hill country of Judea as "the blessed one." She spent much time with the Lord, pouring out to Him her heart of thankfulness. The ache of barrenness. . .gone! O, praise the Lord, she was barren no more!

She was nearing her sixth month when her young cousin Mary from Nazareth arrived at her home. Elizabeth had not expected her visit, for it was nearly four days' journey from Nazareth to Hebron where they lived, a distance of almost one hundred miles. But, from the moment she saw Mary, she knew that something even more wonderful than her miracle had happened. At the sound of Mary's voice, her baby leaped in her womb as if in exaltation. The little one inside her literally jumped for joy! She was so overwhelmed by the wonder of the moment, she didn't even notice the ache under her ribs.

Elizabeth felt her heart filled with a joy that she knew could only come from the Spirit of the Living God. Suddenly, she knew! She knew what only Mary had known before. Mary was going to be the mother of the Messiah! God's Savior would be born to her!

"Blessed are you among women, and blessed is the Child you will bear! But why am I so favored, that the mother of my Lord shall come to me? As soon as the sound of your greeting reached my ears, the baby in my womb leaped for joy! Blessed is she who has believed what the Lord has said to her will be accomplished!"

The look on Mary's face showed great relief. "Oh, Elizabeth! I knew God would reassure me through you! He told me through an angel that you were going to have a baby. When I heard of your miracle, I found it easier to believe Him for the miracle He is doing in me as well. Somehow, I knew you would understand." Relieved, she fell into Elizabeth's arms and Elizabeth held her close to her heart.

She felt the Lord holding them both very close to His heart as well.

The two spent nearly three months together, precious time for the two mothers-to-be. They talked of the things expectant mothers talk about— making clothes, feeding babies, morning sickness, the miracle of life growing in their wombs.

They did not talk about names for their sons, however, for both babies had already been named. . . by God.

From the solid, faithful, loving heart of Elizabeth, Mary gained the encouragement and wisdom she would need to handle the months ahead. She too would be whispered about among the women. She too would face days of wondering just what all these divinely ordained events would mean. With gentleness and humility, Elizabeth ministered to her young cousin, who was barely a teenager. Elizabeth knew that her child would never be as important as Mary's, yet she poured her love into the young woman's life.

In Elizabeth's ninth month, and Mary's third, Mary left to return to her Joseph in Nazareth. The two women clung to each other in a long embrace before Mary turned to leave.

"Thank you, thank you," Mary whispered.

"I'll be praying for you. . .I love you," Elizabeth softly said in return.

They would not see each other again until both their sons were born.

Finally, for Zechariah and Elizabeth, the great day came! Zechariah paced nervously. Elizabeth rested between contractions. Then, as the pain increased and became more frequent, her attention completely focused on the birth. She grimaced, sweat running down her face, taking deep breaths. One more push. . .

the sound of a baby crying. . .

her baby!

John had come at last! Zechariah leaned over her as Elizabeth lay exhausted and kissed her gently. Their tears of joy mingled together as their son took his first meal from his mother.

Thank God for Elizabeths! They are the quiet people who are often unnoticed. Yet, when God wants to do something important, they are often an integral part of His plan. People like Elizabeth remind us that God's way of rewarding faithfulness doesn't always fit into our sense of timing. But His way of vindicating our reputation is always better than ours, for when we humbly trust Him, God knows how to take our barrenness and turn it into miraculous blessedness. Not positioned by God to be in the limelight, Elizabeth, nonetheless, gave her wholehearted encouragement to Mary so God's spotlight could shine brightly on the mother of God. Because "the consecrated one" saw her child as a gift from God, she was willing to put John in God's hands to cooperate with His purposes. She was willing to help prepare the way for the Savior of the world.

Her son would do the same.

Keith Mueller

The Man God Trusted to Raise His Son

He walked down the path from his carpenter's shop to Mary's house, the sun warm on his face, the breeze carrying the bright sounds of a songbird to his ears. Breathing deeply the fresh air of late spring, he exhaled slowly, smiling up into the sky. Life was good! He was engaged to the most wonderful girl in the world! In just a few months they would be married. . .he could hardly wait. He had worked hard on the small house they would share as husband and wife. With her woman's touch, Mary would soon turn it into a home of love and happiness. He smiled to himself again. . .someday he would have to enlarge the house to accommodate their children. Yes, God was being good to him. The gift of a wife was more than Joseph could have ever dreamed.

It had been three months since he had seen Mary. He was eager to see her face again, hear her voice again, be near her again. She had gone to visit her cousin Elizabeth, who was expecting a baby. Elizabeth was well past childbearing age, but several months ago miraculous news came from Hebron that surprised and amazed them all. The old couple would have to prepare a nursery! Not long after the news about Elizabeth had come, Mary left rather suddenly. Although Joseph couldn't seem to place the feeling, he had a sense that something had happened to Mary that had changed her. Still, he was eager to see her again, as soon as possible!

When he got near Mary's home, her little brothers and sisters ran to greet him on the path, shouting his name, smiling up at him, and grabbing his hand. Joseph laughed and threw one of the boys on his strong shoulders as he neared the door. Looking into the house, he saw Mary rise from where she was sitting and come to meet him. There was something different about her! He noticed a glow on her face and a quiet depth in her eyes he had not noticed before. . .but her voice still carried the familiar ring

of joy when she said his name.

"Joseph!" She ran to him, eagerly taking him by both hands, looking up into his face, her eyes shining. Joseph fell in love all over again, looking into those beautiful eyes.

For a few minutes they made small talk with Mary's father and mother—talking of the weather, of how Joseph's business was coming along. . .all the common things people talk of with the familiarity of family.

Joseph was but a young man, just past his twentieth year, but in their culture he was of age to marry and expected to support himself. Being a carpenter was a good trade, one he had learned from his own father, but probably not one that would make him wealthy. Their area was not heavily forested, so good wood was hard to find. People built their homes with little wood, relying instead on stone and clay mortar. Furniture made of wood was often unavailable except for the wealthy.

The life of a carpenter was not an easy one, but Joseph had worked hard to become a master craftsman. He had big dreams for his business and family. Mary's parents knew they were getting a steady, stable young man, more serious than most his age, as a son-in-law. Joseph also had an uncommon sensitivity to spiritual things. He was a man who sought to honor God by his actions more than just his words. They knew Mary could have done much worse than Joseph for a husband. Soon he would be an official part of the family, and that made them glad.

At last, Joseph and Mary rose to take a walk so they could talk alone together. Outside the village, they found a peaceful place that looked out across the valley. For a long while, they were quiet, Mary's head resting on his shoulder. Mary turned to him, looking deep into Joseph's eyes.

And then she told him.

The words hit harder than if someone had struck him over the head with one of his carpenter's mallets. At first he was numb, unable to comprehend what she really meant. The words were so unexpected, so seemingly impossible, that he was speechless. As the full weight of Mary's words filtered past his mind and into his heart, it seemed his whole world was crashing down around him.

"Joseph. . .I'm going to have a baby."

A baby? Mary, his beloved, his intended Mary? It couldn't be! Could it? Not from him at least. They had remained pure. . .saving themselves for marriage.

And now this.

Her words could only mean one thing. . .Mary had been unfaithful to him. The ultimate act of betrayal. . .the one thing he thought could never happen to him.

Joseph suddenly felt weak, his stomach churning. His mind still could not grasp what had happened. This was the woman he loved. She was the one! He had committed his life and love to her completely. . .to be faithful to her alone. What was happening?

Mary knelt down in front of him, her eyes filled with tears, her hands resting on his callused carpenter's hands. "Joseph. . .it's not what you think. I haven't been unfaithful to you. I'm still a virgin. . .but I'm going to have a baby."

Joseph looked up at her, his eyes filled with confusion. "Still a virgin? Yet you are going to have a baby? Mary, that's impossible!"

Mary nodded in agreement and urgency. "Yes, it is impossible. . .but not with God, Joseph. Nothing is impossible with God. God sent an angel to me. . .and the Baby within me is the One He promised He would send us. Joseph, the Son I will bear is the Son of God. God has chosen me to be the mother of the Messiah." Her face glowed. In hushed, reverent tones she told him of Gabriel's incredible visit. She spoke of Elizabeth's affirmation: The Child Mary carried was truly the Christ.

Joseph had never, ever known Mary to be dishonest with him before. . .but this was so improbable that it was unbelievable. She must have met someone while she was visiting Elizabeth. She couldn't have willingly. . .

someone must have forced her to. . .

No!

NO!

This couldn't be! They loved each other. They had kept themselves pure, although the temptation to give in to their passions had been strong at times. Now Mary was asking him to believe a story like this. . . .

He listened to her, his mind too numb to even ask questions. He wanted to, but he couldn't get the words to come out of his mouth. They died on his lips, even as he felt his dreams dying in his heart. He sat there in stunned silence, looking at her with eyes blurred with tears of pain and bewilderment. The enormity of the dilemma completely overwhelmed him. Finally, he walked her back to her house and then stumbled down the path to his.

He found himself standing in a daze in front of his house. His house. . .it was to have been their home. Joseph had worked so hard preparing this simple home for them to share as husband and wife. This was where they were to live together—to share their dreams, their hardships, their routines, their meals, and their bed together.

What now?

All those wonderful dreams had become a nightmare. In their small village of Nazareth there would be gossip. . .scandal. . .the embarrassment of sly looks and snide comments from people as he walked by. . .the stigma of being a man whose wife-to-be had been unfaithful to him. His heart felt like a board suddenly snapped in pieces, the jagged splinters stabbing him with pain like he had never felt before. These splinters of betrayal had punctured his very soul.

He thought he might vomit. He clenched and unclenched his fists, not knowing what to do with them. Finally, he threw himself down on his bed and wept the deep, heaving, pain-filled sobs of a man whose dreams have ended before they ever really began.

After a long time, he could weep no more. His head ached, his eyes hurt. He sat on the edge of his bed, holding his head in his hands. What now? *Think,* he said to himself, *you've got to think.*

Think!

What could he do? Desperately he cried out, "Oh God, where are You?" What could the Lord have to say that could help him now? Joseph had always sought to live in line with God's laws. His heart was fully devoted to the Lord, but when the heart is crushed, sometimes God's voice is hard to hear. From deep within an anguished heart, his pleading groans sought something. . . anything from the Almighty to help him know what to do.

His mind recalled what the Law said about the sin of adultery. The options were few—he could publicly expose her guilt and have her put to death by stoning. Joseph shuddered at the thought of his Mary, broken and bloody, dead beneath a hailstorm of sharp rocks. No, even if Mary was guilty of adultery, he could never bring himself to allow that to happen to her.

What else? He could divorce her—all he needed to do was write up the divorce document and hand it to her in the presence of two witnesses. Their relationship would be over, but Mary's life would be spared.

What should he do? Joseph wanted to do what God wanted. He knew God was a God of mercy, not only of judgment. What would God want him to do, even in the face of such betrayal? He thought of the stories of others who had been betrayed. Hosea the prophet's wife had borne him children, then left him for the life of a prostitute. God told Hosea to forgive his unfaithful wife and even restored their marriage. In the scroll of Isaiah, God Himself compared His relationship with Israel to a husband betrayed by an unfaithful wife. He was the Faithful Husband, heartbroken, longing for His relationship with His beloved to be restored.

For a long time Joseph stared into space. . .thinking. . .praying. The course of his life hung on this moment like a hinge. What he would choose would open doors affecting not only his life but Mary's. . .and the Baby's. As he pondered, his mind came to a point of understanding and his heart to a point of decision. He would do the right thing. He would show Mary mercy. Perhaps. . .perhaps God would bring him another wife. . .someday.

Exhausted by the strain of the day and the decision, he fell into turbulent sleep. Some time later, in the midst of his restless slumber, he was suddenly aware of a presence. The room glowed with light unlike any he'd ever seen. Joseph was conscious of something supernatural there with him.

What was it? An angel? Angel! Could it really be? It was just as Mary had described happening to her! God had sent him a messenger just as He had to Mary! It was a dream—but it was also an experience of supernatural reality for Joseph.

The messenger spoke, his voice deep yet reassuring. "Joseph, son of David, do not be afraid to take Mary as your wife. The Baby she is carrying is indeed from God. You are to give Him the name Jesus, for He shall save His people from their sins."

With that, the messenger was gone. The room returned to normal again.

Joseph woke instantly, looking around, his eyes wide with wonder. So it was true! It was just as Mary had said! God was trusting his beloved Mary to give birth to the Son of God. . .and God was trusting him to be the man who would raise His Son. Him. Joseph of Nazareth! Slowly he let it all sink in. . .and the reassuring peace of God filled his heart. His dreams were not destroyed after all. . . no, God was fulfilling them beyond his farthest expectations! As he sat in silent wonder, another passage from the scroll of Isaiah came to his heart:

Therefore the Lord Himself will give you a sign: The virgin will be with child and will give birth to a Son and will call him Immanuel. . .For to us a Child is born, to us a Son is given, and the government shall be on His shoulders. And He will be called Wonderful, Counselor, Mighty God, Everlasting Father, Prince of Peace.

It was really happening! God was going to send His Son, the Messiah, to reside with His people, to redeem them and to ultimately reign over all creation. Joseph was overwhelmed again, this time with awe instead of anguish. He knelt at the side of his bed, his face lifted to heaven, and the tears that streamed down his face now were the tears of a joy-filled man. Out of a heart overcome with worship and wonder he poured out praise to such an awesome, faithful God. As he lifted his rough carpenter's hands in worship, he felt as though the Almighty God reached down and grasped them. God Himself would lead Joseph into the days ahead.

The hearts of two fathers, the eternal heavenly Father and the humble earthly father, communed as one.

He could barely wait until the first light of morning to run all the way to Mary's house, take her in his arms, and kiss her right there in front of her family, declaring his love for her forever. Their tears mingled as he told her of his amazing visit from God's messenger. They traded stories about their supernatural visits, nodding and laughing at the sheer wonder of God's incredible plan for their lives.

That plan was greater than they could have ever imagined. Two lives whose expectations only went to the edges of Nazareth would now have an influence that would extend to the ends of the earth and to the end of time. Only God. . . only God could arrange something so incredible, and they were glad He was allowing them to live it together. Together they would face their future as husband and wife. Together they would raise the One who would change the course of all humanity. Together, with God's guiding wisdom and love, they would face the challenges of what people would say about them.

Together. . .with God.

As he walked back to his carpenter's shop, something was different about Joseph. When God puts His hand on an ordinary life and gives it supernatural purpose, the change is obvious. Joseph's eyes were bright, his heart clear, his shoulders square, his steps sure. This simple carpenter from Nazareth, this man who sought with all his heart to honor God, was given an honor by God unlike any other in all of history.

This was the man God trusted to raise His Son.

The Price of a Room

*H*e sighed as he wiped his hands on a greasy towel. *Too much to do, too little time to do it,* he thought. Amos' day, already too long, wasn't finished yet. As innkeeper of Bethlehem's only inn, he was a very public, very pressured, and not always very popular man. He didn't take pride in his position at the moment.

Usually it wasn't so bad. Bethlehem was just a small village high on a ridge a scant six miles from the capital city of Jerusalem. As such, it received little notice. Travelers normally made Bethlehem a last stopping place before the final leg of a journey ending in Jerusalem. The spotlight of political, economic, and spiritual attention was always focused on Jerusalem, with Bethlehem barely noticed on the dim edges. For the great majority of people, Bethlehem rated little attention, if any. It was but an insignificant moon in the orbit of Jerusalem's sun.

Until now.

Although present-day Bethlehem was of little consequence, its past once brought it prominence. Every Israelite knew the origins of their nation. Bethlehem had birthed some of the more well-known people in Jewish national history. The tomb of Rachel, wife of the patriarch Jacob, was near the village in one of the many caves that honeycombed the ridge on which Bethlehem was built. Ruth, the Moabite woman who became famous for her commitment to her mother-in-law when death took the men in their family, married Boaz of Bethlehem and raised a family there. Three generations later, the most famous of all people identified with Bethlehem, King David, grew up shepherding sheep in the surrounding hills. At Bethlehem the prophet Samuel anointed David king of the nation. Bethlehem, which meant "House of Bread," became known as "the city of David." Micah the prophet even made a prediction about the little town, declaring it to be the place where God's Messiah would be born:

But you, Bethlehem Ephrathah, though you are small, too little to be listed among the clans of Judah, out of you will come for Me One who will be ruler over Israel, whose origins are from old, from ancient time. . .He will stand and shepherd His flock in the strength of the Lord, in the majesty of the name of the Lord His God. And they will live securely, for then His greatness will reach to the ends of the earth. And He will be their peace.

It was a powerful prediction at the time. The hometown of the nation's most famous shepherd king would be the birthplace of the King of the Universe! From the "shepherd's hills" of little Bethlehem, One would emerge as a Shepherd to an entire world. However, as the years, decades, and centuries passed, both Bethlehem's former glory and prophetic future faded until it receded into a sleepy village on the hilly outskirts of Jerusalem.

Until now.

The politics of the region had always been volatile, and currently the Romans ruled the region, overseeing an uneasy peace. Unrest always simmered under the surface. The Romans had done much for the infrastructure of the land—building roads, aqueducts, and other public works projects—but all of that came for a price. Taxes steadily consumed a growing portion of every family's income. . .and where there are oppressive taxes, there are unhappy people. Still, there was little a person could do but pay the government and do the best he could with Roman leftovers.

The most recent edict delivered in the name of Caesar Augustus mandated a census be taken of the entire inhabited world under Roman rule. Since the Jews identified themselves by the hometowns of their families of origin, all the descendants of a particular family tree had to return to their roots and register. A census completion meant, of course, more tax collection.

Because Bethlehem was the ancestral hometown of the line of David, a huge influx of travelers claiming royal blood in their veins flowed into the area, clogging every conceivable dwelling place. Every traveler, from far and near, needed a place to eat, rest, and take care of their furry transportation. That was what made Amos such a sought-after and stressed-out man.

He sighed again as he looked over the courtyard of his inn. Like many in their land, it was a rectangular, flat-roofed building of many small rooms opening to a courtyard in the middle. In the middle of the courtyard patrons all drew their water from a common well. Some of the small rooms had stalls in them for an animal to stay with the family. Sometimes people slept in the open courtyard if there was no vacancy anywhere else. Few could afford one of the better rooms. Amos allowed his customers to cook their own food over the fire in the courtyard, or he provided meals for a price. Fodder for the animals was also supplied. The inn was not a place with much privacy or comfort. It was primitive, but it was all Bethlehem had to offer travelers with no friend or family to accommodate them.

Amos and his family had but a small room of their own at the inn, but since the caravans of travelers began to arrive, he had had no chance to even be home in his small place. This was the week of census registration. *And,* he thought wryly, *the week of my frustration.* Well, after all, he remembered, his name meant "burden bearer"—and this week the burdens of his business weighed so heavily on him that he felt a sluggish sympathy with the staggering burro he'd seen this afternoon bearing a bulging man into his courtyard. He grimaced at the memory.

He did not pretend to understand all the political implications preceding the invasion of his inn, nor did he want to. His involvement with politics included only the banter he knew was expected of him as a genial host. Amos had too much to worry about without getting involved in politics or religion. He was not against Caesar or God, mind you, it was just that more immediate things demanded his attention.

Still, Amos couldn't help catching the conversations around the fires as people reminisced about Bethlehem's past. They speculated about Micah's prophecies and reflected on the four hundred years of divine silence since. No miracles. No messages from God. People yearned for freedom in a land ruled by Roman might. They hungered for peace in a time where the whim of a Roman ruler threw their world into upheaval. They wondered if God even knew their plight. . .did He still care?

Would He ever send His Messiah to deliver them as He'd promised?

Amos had joined in the conversations when he felt he was required to, but mostly he had listened. The tone of these conversations, Amos noticed dimly, was different from the routine reports of people resting from a day on the road. A few wondered aloud if this great regathering of people to Bethlehem was more than just a Roman policy. Perhaps it was part of a greater plan of God. Such talk grabbed his attention briefly, but soon the request of another guest of the inn demanded his attention, and any thoughts of God were gone.

Amos considered himself to be like many people. He wasn't against God. . .he believed in Him and had a sense of respect for things spiritual, but he just never seemed to have enough time to really get serious about religion. There was an inn to run with guests to please, orders to fill, bills to pay, suppliers to work with. . .and something was always in need of repair. Then there were his wife and children. His children were growing so fast! It seemed that he got to spend so little time with them. He and his wife worked hard together, but they were usually too busy to really spend the kind of time that makes a marriage strong and satisfying. Beyond that, there never seemed to be any time for Amos to enjoy by himself. Amos bore plenty of burdens, and he felt he was doing well if he was getting through one day and into the next. Taking time to think about God was a luxury he could rarely afford. The urgent always seemed to crowd out the important.

Occasionally, after a long day, Amos gazed up into a night sky with the stars twinkling down on him, and he wondered if a God that could make such a huge universe could care personally about an average working man like him. He even tried praying sometimes, and there were times when he felt a peculiar sense of. . .a kind of peace. It felt good to try to tell God about what was on his mind, especially if things were tight and he needed help. Rarely, however, did he take time to listen to what God might say back to him.

The stars were twinkling down on him now, evidence that night had come to the inn at last. What a day! Every bit of available space was rented. The large courtyard was so full of people sleeping out in the open that it was hard to walk among them without stepping on someone. He had already turned many people away, leaving them to find their own food and lodging. He knew the majority of them would be sleeping in the fields surrounding the city and shivering in the winter air, but there was little he could do. He had too much to worry about without trying to deal with the problems of other people.

He stretched his arms above his head, trying to take the ache out of some of his overused muscles. His back was sore, his feet ached, his stomach was growling from not having time to eat, and he just wanted to get some rest. Tugging on his bushy beard, he rubbed his eyes as he gazed once more over the crowded scene in front of him.

Some still sat up talking around the fires. Others tried to get some sleep, overcome by exhaustion from the exertion of the journey. He hoped there would be no squabbling over sleeping space like he had to deal with last night. Trying to play peacemaker to overtired patrons was a thankless and sleepless job. He couldn't handle too many more nights like that. Silently he breathed a wishful prayer for things to remain peaceful. Turning toward his room, he trudged to his door and stepped inside.

His children were already sleeping. His wife wearily gave him some leftovers from the evening meal of bread, cheese, and dried figs. Conversation was sparse, more from their fatigue than anything else. The dim light from their small lamp deepened the lines exhaustion had etched on their faces. With one more long sigh, Amos turned in for the night, leaving the greasy towel hanging on a peg by the doorway.

He had not been sleeping long (at least it felt like he had just shut his eyes) when he heard a tentative tapping at their doorway. The lure of sleep made everything inside of him want to turn over and ignore the knock. Maybe whoever it was would go away. The night was quiet for a moment. Then the knocking came again, a bit louder this time. His wife, always a lighter sleeper than he was, nudged him in the side with her elbow, and with a groan Amos rolled up to a sitting position and struggled to his feet. Still unsteady with sleep, he wobbled to the door and stepped out into the crisp night air.

In front of him stood a young man, and even in the moonlight Amos could tell he was barely twenty. It was obvious that the young man had been traveling all day from the dust that covered him and the weariness in his eyes. But there was something else in those eyes that drew Amos' attention, a pleading look that let Amos know he was encountering something out of the ordinary.

"Please, sir," the young man's voice was low but insistent. "My name is Joseph, and this is my wife Mary. We have been traveling five days from Nazareth. . .my wife is about to have a child. . .and the pains have begun." As the young man spoke, he turned to look at where the gate opened into the courtyard just a few feet from Amos' door.

There at the gate, a young woman stood leaning against the side of a small burro. She was obviously great with child. Her head hung down from sheer exhaustion, but when she heard her husband speak of her, she lifted her head to look up at Amos. In the moonlight he saw the face of a young woman who could not be much more than fifteen or sixteen years old. Her face was drawn, a light sheen of perspiration showing she was definitely in labor. She grimaced and bent over, breathing hard as another contraction came. . .and Amos could see the pleading in her eyes, too.

Obviously this young couple were new to entering parenthood. Just as obviously they were in great need of help. In spite of the urgency of the situation, they were not in a panic, though. Somehow Amos got the feeling that they were being watched over in a way he could not describe.

"Please, sir," the young man spoke again. "I know it is very late, but we must have a room, a place where my wife can give birth. We thank God that He has brought us safely this far. Can you help us?"

Amos had been in a position to turn away many potential customers over the course of time, but this was a situation unlike any he had ever experienced. This young woman was about to give birth on his doorstep! His mind, dull with sleep just a moment ago, now swiftly tried to figure out what to do. He couldn't have her stay out in the open courtyard. . .it would be too cold for her and too noisy for the others trying to sleep. There were no rooms available, that was for sure

. . .unless

. . .unless Amos gave them his room.

His room would be a safe, warm place to bring the child into the world. But what would he do with his family? It would be such an inconvenience to wake them all up, move them, and get to sleep again, especially for the children. *Wait a minute,* his mind told him. . .*there's another possibility.*

Behind the inn, just down the hill, was a cave. Hollowed out of the soft limestone by time, water, wind, and human effort, it was big enough to be used as a stable. There were several animals there, but the cave would be somewhat warm from their heat, there would be fresh straw for use as a delivery bed, and there would be a measure of privacy.

It just might work.

The question was, for who?

The thought of a baby being born in a rocky barn made him uncomfortable. Surely this baby deserved to be born in a place better than the stable. He knew the best place for Joseph and Mary was in his own room. His wife could help with the delivery, he could take the children to her parents' home, and he could sleep in the stable.

But. . .

But to get his family up, to lose even more sleep trying to doze in the stable, to get the children dressed again. . .it was just too much of an inconvenience. He'd had too much stress already for one day; it would just be easier to put the couple in the barn, baby or no.

Mary groaned softly and bent over in pain as another contraction came. She looked at the two men, her eyes large. "Joseph," she said, panting. "Please. . .the baby. . ." Joseph turned to look at Amos, the pleading look again on his face.

Amos had to choose. His room, or the stable? His heart told him the right thing, but over-ruling his heart, he shook his head and whispered, "I'm sorry. There is no room here at the inn. But. . .there is a place you can use. Wait just a moment." Quickly, Amos ducked back inside his home and grabbed the lamp. Lighting it, he led the couple with their burro down the hill to the stable. Standing before the entrance, he pointed inside and said, "It's warm, dry, there is straw, and you will have some privacy. You can keep the lamp. I will bring you some water from the well. . . but this is the best I can do."

Even as he said the words, Amos knew it wasn't true, but he squelched his conscience. Joseph seemed greatly relieved and gripped Amos' shoulder with a quiet gesture of thanks. Mary, moving as quickly as she could, took the cloak Joseph offered her and headed for a place to lie down in the straw. The baby would at least be born with a roof over His head.

When he finished bringing the couple a jug of water, Amos struggled slowly back up the hill to his own warm home and lay back down next to his sleeping wife. He did not go to sleep right away, though. He lay on his back, staring up into the darkness. There had been something unusual about the whole incident, something he couldn't place his finger on. What was it? Joseph mentioned God helping them on their journey. Did God have something to do with this?

The prophecy of Micah flashed through his mind. . .could it be?

No. . .not here. Not now. Not like this. A King would be born in a palace, not at a nonde-script inn like his, and certainly not in a stable. Still. . .there was something more going on than met the natural eye. Amos pondered those possibilities, but then sleep overtook him again.

It was, he thought just as he drifted off, *nice to be in his own bed.*

While he slept, the greatest birth in human history took place just feet away. The miracle of the birth of Jesus Christ could have taken place in his own home if he had chosen to allow it. But Amos missed the opportunity to see God do a miracle in his own life. . .a miracle as close as his own doorstep, but he had been too preoccupied to notice. His life was just so full there was no room for

Jesus to be born there. Instead he gave Christ the little extra room he thought he could afford—not at the heart of his home and life, but out back and out of the way.

Life-changing choices are often disguised as ordinary decisions. Many people are like Amos, bearing life's burdens, feeling overwhelmed by the stresses of trying to scrape by, much less succeed in life. God is often much closer than we realize, if we'd take the time to notice Him at work right near us. He is waiting to bring us the miracle of spiritual birth, the supernatural wonder of seeing Jesus make Himself at home in our own life.

Yes, Jesus brings changes that we may not initially think are convenient, but in the long run these changes become indispensable. Yet, like Amos, we are so busy. . .too busy for the King of the Universe to take His rightful place on the throne of our hearts. We may not feel we are opposing the Lord, but it is all too easy to allow other "urgent" things to be more important. These seemingly essential issues crowd the Master out of actively influencing our lives. In so choosing we show where our true loyalties lie.

Oftentimes the Lord comes to us in ways we do not expect. The nudge we feel in our hearts is the whisper of His Spirit beckoning us to discover the miracle just behind the mundane. Too often, our minds, frazzled by the rush of life, overrule the voice we hear speaking to our heart. . .and God is moved to the back of our lives, out of the way again.

For Amos, the price of a room that Christmas Eve cost him more than he could have ever realized. It was the price of missing out on the miracle of Christ's birth—and God's best for Amos and his family. For us, the "price of a room" is also much more than we can ever humanly calculate. It is the price we pay when we choose not to open our hearts to Jesus Christ. It is the price of missing God's best.

There's Someone knocking at the door of your heart.

Have you any room?

Through Angels' Eyes

They floated high above the Judean landscape, their wings fluttering gently, radiantly beautiful. Far below them, the darkness was broken only by the lights that twinkled from a village, as well as a few solitary dots from the campfires of shepherds in the hills. Over to their right, about six miles away, were the brighter lights of a large city, Jerusalem, the capital of Israel.

However, the attention of the two angels focused on the little town of Bethlehem. Gabriel turned to his fellow archangel Michael with a look of eagerness and delight. "Tonight is the night, is it not?" he said, more a statement of confirmation than a question.

"Yes." Michael nodded. "Our Lord has brought together the events of this night according to His perfect plan. The Son of God is about to enter human history as a baby."

Gabriel's eyes gleamed as he turned again to look down at the earth below. "It has been so fascinating watching the great plan of God come together. The Promise He gave Adam and Eve in the Garden. He saved Noah and his family on the Ark when the whole world was warped by sin. What mercy! We watched Him choose Abraham to share His covenant and make him the father of the faithful. Giving Sarah and him a son in their advanced age was such a joyful event. Raising up Israel, a nation that would bless all the other nations of the world through their descendants, set His course for history. The revelation His Spirit gave the prophets so they could tell about the coming of the Son of God. The Lord God has orchestrated the rise and fall of governments to set the world stage. He has taken care of all the details, even down to the building of good roads for Mary to travel on to get to Bethlehem. Truly humanity will look back on all this and marvel at the Lord's sovereign planning."

Michael smiled. "It is amazing to me how much the Lord God loves them. He gave them everything in creation to enjoy. He is even willing to forgive them and make them a part of His family. Yet most of these humans act as if He does not even exist. They break His laws, spurn His love, try to make themselves into little gods and fail miserably. They are turning His beautiful creation into a shambles. Still, in spite of their rebellion against His love. . .this incredible plan to redeem and restore them!" He pointed toward Bethlehem. "And there, the greatest evidence of His love. . .God the Son is actually going to go down and become one of them. . .live among them . . . die for them."

Gabriel's face hardened. "Yes, but our enemy and his forces will do all they can to stop Him. They have been deceiving and destroying people since the Garden, and they will come against the Son and His followers more than anyone else. We've been in constant conflict with our enemy and his forces ever since they rebelled against the Lord God. We have fought them on every level—Lucifer has demon forces seeking to control nations, governments, cities, families, and individual lives."

The two angels were quiet for a moment, reflecting on the intense battles the armies of heaven had fought against Lucifer's forces over the course of many of earth's centuries. Though invisible, these conflicts had influenced the direction and destiny of untold numbers of human beings.

"Even though his only power is in deception, our adversary controls the minds of far too many." Gabriel's voice showed the strain of his sadness. "How little these humans realize what violent events go on around them in the realm of the spirit! Their eternal souls are at stake. They are the prize in battles with eternal consequences. Someday we will see our enemy vanquished forever. For now, however, we must be ever vigilant to serve and protect those the Lord God loves."

He pointed to Jerusalem. "Satan has a real stronghold there. King Herod is in his grip, little more than a puppet in his hands. The religious leaders are blinded by their own traditions and pride. Even now our enemy is maneuvering Herod into trying to kill the Son soon after His birth."

Michael nodded gravely. "The battle will be fierce, but thanks be to God that we shall have victory. The Lord Jesus will come and carry out His plan to save all those who will come to Him by faith. We will be working, unseen, but with the prayer support of God's people, we will continue to overcome our enemy's forces. Are the guards in place around Mary and Joseph?"

"Yes, our best are with them, although it seems no one else is. There was no room for them in the inn. How could that innkeeper turn away a woman about to deliver a baby? They are safe in a stable just down the hill from the inn. It's a cave that will keep them sheltered from the wind and chill and provide some soft hay for Mary and the baby." Gabriel's expression grew sad. "The King of the Universe entering into their world, and He suffers the most impoverished birth. I know He wanted to identify with them, but to this degree?"

Michael put his hand on his friend's shoulder. "Don't forget, my brother, how far God's love is willing to go when it comes to those made in His image."

From above them, a deep and regal voice spoke. "Gabriel. Michael."

Instantly the two sped back to heaven and knelt before the throne of God, covering their faces in humility with their shining wings. "Yes, Lord?" they said.

"The time has come." The Father's face was radiant. "I have one more announcement for you to make, Gabriel. Michael, call the choir that regularly ministers around the throne and take them with you. I want those shepherds to hear the music of Heaven so they understand who My Son is. They are guarding the lambs for sacrifice in the Temple. Tell them about the Lamb of God who will take away the sins of the world. They will be the first to know."

The two angels stood, their wings full and shimmering with iridescent beauty. "It will be our great delight, Lord!" they said, and with another bow, they were gone.

Gabriel flew low until he hovered just a few feet above the shepherds. They recoiled in

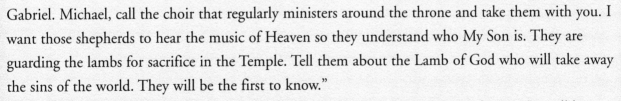

stunned fear, but he raised his hand in greeting and smiled.

"Do not be afraid. I bring you good news of great joy that will be for all the people. Today in the town of David a Savior has been born to you. He is Messiah, the Lord. This will be a sign to you: You will find a baby wrapped in strips of cloth and lying in a manger."

With Gabriel's announcement, the radiance of the angels seemed to intensify. Wave after wave of glory bathed the shepherds until they fell to their knees, overwhelmed with wonder. Then, with a signal from Michael, the choir began to sing. Such harmony, such majestic melody had never been heard on the earth. This was the music of the throne room of Heaven, sung to a small band of simple shepherds.

"Glory to God in the highest, and on earth peace to those on whom His favor rests!"

The divine concert continued on as all the pent up joy of the angels was released to the universe. The Son of God is born! The Savior is come! Our Lord is here among humanity! Glory to God! Glory to God!

At last the angelic chorale finished their Christmas concert. Michael took the choir back to Heaven, but Gabriel still hovered in the night sky, watching as the shepherds made their way into the village.

He saw them find their way at last to the stable outside the inn. Invisible to human eyes, the angels guarding the door stood aside so they could go in, and Gabriel followed them.

The shepherds spoke with Mary and Joseph, and then they fell to their knees. Gabriel looked at their bent heads for a moment, thinking what rough, small creatures these humans were, so blind, so limited. . .and so loved by God. He looked over their shoulders at the King of Creation, lying in manger straw. The almighty Son of God had wrapped Himself in the swaddling cloth of human flesh.

And Gabriel knelt with them.

"Do not be afraid. I bring you good news of great joy that will be for all the people. Today in the town of David a Savior has been born to you; he is Christ the Lord. This will be a sign to you: You will find a baby wrapped in cloths and lying in a manger."

Luke 2:10-12 NIV

The Gift of Joy

The night air carried winter's chill. Trying to ward off its effects, Benjamin drew his shepherd's cloak around him more tightly. He sighed deeply, and could see his breath. Across the valley, up on a ridge a half mile away, he could see a few lights from the village of Bethlehem. There most of the people were warm and asleep in their homes, while Benjamin was cold and awake out here in the fields. Only the stars, the sheep, and his fellow shepherds kept him company. The sheep were bedded down for the night, and soft snores told him that some of his fellow shepherds had done so, too.

Benjamin sighed again. He didn't like it when he was here at night by himself. During the day he could laugh and joke with the others and act as if all was well, but the solitude and darkness of the night seemed to intensify the restlessness in his heart. Something was missing. . .something that he had been secretly seeking for a long time. What was it? Happiness? No, that wasn't quite the right word. He was happy or sad depending on the circumstances around him, but he was hungry for something deeper, more powerful than just the temporary highs of good feelings. He wanted something not dependent on what was going on around him. What Benjamin yearned for was something more than a feeling. So. . .what was it, then? He just couldn't seem to put his finger on it, but when he found it, he knew he'd recognize it.

He heard approaching footsteps, and turned to see his brother Joshua walking toward him in the moonlight. Joshua, older by a few years, seemed to know when Benjamin needed to talk. Though they did not express it often, a deep bond was between them.

"Thinking, my brother?" Joshua asked. "You've got that look on your face again. What's on your mind? It's either that girl in Bethlehem or you're trying to figure out what to do with your share of the money when we sell the sheep. Am I right?"

Benjamin looked at his brother and smiled. "You are usually right, brother," he said, "but not this time. No. . .I was thinking of other things. Sometimes I guess I think too much."

"So. . . .what were you thinking of, then?" Joshua's voice was playful and yet inquisitive. "Looking to the stars to find the answers to life?"

"No, I've looked at those stars for too long to think there's any help from them. I don't know if there's any help at all from above."

"Now that's a surprising thing to say, Benjamin. Here we are, shepherds who have the privilege of guarding sheep that will go to the temple to be the sacrifices for the forgiveness of our sins. Don't you don't think God in Heaven cares about you?"

Benjamin's voice had an edge of bitterness as he spoke. "Come on, Joshua. You know as well as I do that those religious leaders in the temple think we're good enough to watch over these sheep, but not good enough to come in the temple and take part in their worship. They say we are unclean because we smell of sheep, because our hands are rough, because there's dirt under our fingernails. Just because we can't keep all their rules doesn't mean they should shut us out from God!" He paused, breathing heavily, caught up in the emotion of his words.

"Besides, I'm not sure God even knows we're here. . .and if He does, I'm not sure He even cares about us. He'll probably strike me down for saying such things, but it's hard to feel that Someone you can't even see could care about you."

Joshua was silent for a moment, not sure how to respond to his brother's outburst. True, as shepherds they were looked down upon by some of the so-called "good" people. The sheep they took care of were allowed to go farther into the temple than they were. But Benjamin was missing something. . .he was looking at it from the wrong angle. When Joshua spoke, his voice was gentle but it carried the feeling of his conviction. "Some of what you say is true, Ben, but not all of it. God does care about us, poor shepherds though we be. Don't forget His promises. They bring hope and comfort to my heart. Remember His greatest promise—someday He will send us the Messiah. Just because you can't see Him doesn't mean He doesn't know you or love you. He lets us know that in so many ways."

"Well, I'd sure like to have Him show me in a little more obvious way. It's been four hundred years since we've heard the voice of God through angel or prophet in our land. There's been no miracle or any other kind of sign. I'm afraid He's forgotten about us—"

Suddenly the night sky lit up, more brilliant than a midday sun shining on fresh snow. The light was dazzling, powerful, intense. . .and yet it had a gentle warmth. Caught by the unexpected burst of radiance, Benjamin and Joshua fell to the ground, overwhelmed. Cries of surprise and confusion reached their ears as the other shepherds woke up, and they were all momentarily blinded by the light. Surprisingly, the sheep did not stir or become restless. They seemed to have an unearthly peace in the midst of the supernatural brilliance.

The shepherds lay stunned for several heartbeats, and then they sensed a presence in front of them. The air seemed to throb with supernatural power. They raised their faces, shielding their eyes, and there before them was the incredible figure of an angel! They had never seen an angel before, but somehow their minds and hearts knew that they were in the presence of a messenger from Almighty God.

Their eyes grew wide, and they hid their faces, hoping the sight would go away, but when they looked again, the angel was still hovering in the air in front of them. The shepherds gathered into a tight huddle, holding on to each other, scared nearly senseless.

"He heard me, Joshua! He heard me! God heard me say those things and He's sent an angel to kill me." Benjamin's voice shook. "I told you He'd strike me dead. . ."

The angel raised his hand, but a smile spread across his face as he spoke in a deep, resonant voice. "Do not be afraid! I bring you good news of great joy that will be for all people."

Don't be afraid? News of joy? The shepherds were stunned and bewildered. The words were not what they had expected at all. The terror began to fade, and a curious wonder took its place.

The angel continued. "Today in the town of David. . . ," he pointed to Bethlehem, ". . . a Savior has been born to you. He is Messiah, the Lord. This will be a sign to you: You will find a baby wrapped in strips of cloth and lying in a manger."

As the angel spoke his wonder-filled message, his glow intensified. Suddenly, as if a curtain had been drawn back, the shepherds saw the whole sky behind him filled with a vast choir of angels. There were thousands upon thousands, all glowing with heavenly radiance. . .and then they began to sing music like none the shepherds had ever heard before. The music vibrated with an exhilarating, unmistakable current of joy. All the shepherds could do was watch in awe, caught up in the power and glory of what was happening in front of them.

At last the music of the angelic choir ended, its echo reverberating in their hearts. The angel who had spoken to them raised his hand in a farewell gesture. . . .and then the angels were gone. The curtain seemed now to be closed. They were alone in the night air. The light of the stars, now visible again, was pale in comparison to the holy splendor they had just experienced.

For a moment they could not speak. All they could do was look around them in amazement, silently asking each other if they had really, truly witnessed a divine spectacle. Then they all began to talk at once, words piling on top of each other as they tried to describe the indescribable.

How can you describe God breaking into your life and turning it completely around?

Finally Joshua raised his hands in a pleading gesture for quiet. "It's obvious what we must do. . .let's go now, right now, straight to Bethlehem to see this thing that has happened, that the Lord has told us about. We must find this Child! We must see with our own eyes God's Promised One!"

Sensing that somehow God had left an angel or two to watch over the sheep, they literally ran up the hills the entire distance into Bethlehem, fueled by their anticipation. When they got into the town, they began asking everyone still awake if they too had seen the angels or heard the music. People looked at them as if they were crazy, but they continued to ask until they found that a man and his very expectant wife had taken up lodging in the stable down the hill from the inn. It surprised them that no better place could be found for a woman about to give birth, but they hurried off without further questions.

Just down the hill, the soft glow of a lamp lighted the cave's entrance, and they found it easily. They hesitated at the door, out of breath and not sure what to do next.

Joshua stepped forward slowly, his voice low. "Hello? Is there anyone in here?"

From the back of the stable a man came, his face glowing with the unmistakable wonder of a new father, his eyes glistening with joy. He looked at the group of men gathered there at the stable entrance, inquisitive but not afraid. "Yes," he said. "I am Joseph, and my wife Mary and newborn Son are here, too. What is it you wish?"

The shepherds looked at each other, clutching each other's arms in their excitement. This was the place! Quickly Joshua told Joseph the story of their heavenly visitors, and Joseph's eyes grew wide with wonder. "Come," he said. "The Child you are looking for is here, lying in the manger, just as you have been told."

They came forward slowly, feeling the warmth of the stable, smelling the mingled scents of animals and hay, and they saw the young mother as she drew the swaddling cloths around a tiny bundle lying in the manger's hay. In the flickering lamplight, her face glowed with a new mother's radiance as she smiled up at them and motioned for them to come closer to see.

There, only His tiny face and dark hair visible, was the Son of God. The Maker of the

Universe had put on a tiny robe of human flesh, and they were among the first allowed to see Him face-to-face. The group looked down at Him, peering over each other's shoulders, their mouths open in awe. Then, as if the thought came to them all at once, they knelt. . .and worshipped their Savior and Lord. It was the only appropriate thing to do. Tears ran unashamedly down the cheeks of the rugged shepherds, dripping off their beards, making smudges in the dusty stable floor. There were no words that could express what they were experiencing, but their eyes mirrored their awe.

It hit Benjamin then. He had thought God was far away. Now he was seeing Him face to face. He had thought God didn't care for him. Now God had singled him out with the other shepherds to be the first to look upon the newborn King. Not the earthly rulers, not the religious leaders, but he, Benjamin, was among the first to see the Christ. God did know him! God did care for him! God did not need to be feared. . .this Child showed him how much God loved him!

Deep within him, as if given by his newfound Savior, he knew he had found what his heart had wanted for so long. It was just what the angel had said it would be. . .joy. That was it! Deeper than a feeling, more exciting than any happiness he had felt, Benjamin tasted real joy for the first time in his life. He knew he'd never settle for anything else again.

Finally, reluctantly, the shepherds left, but there was a spring in their steps and a sparkle in their eyes not there before. In the days and months and years ahead, they would tell and retell their incredible story to all who would listen. Benjamin was among those who shared the Good News about Jesus. It wasn't hard, because he always told the story from an overflowing heart. He'd found his lifelong desire.

In Jesus, Benjamin had discovered the gift of joy.

"*Glory to God in the highest,*
and on earth peace to men
on whom his favor rests."

Luke 2:14 NIV

*P*eace be with you.

My name is Caspar, the name your tradition has given me. I am from a different time and a different place, but I have been asked to share my story with you. This I will gladly do. What I have to tell you has brought hope and light to many generations. I am one of the wisemen who went to see the young King named Jesus shortly after His birth. My life has been transformed by the journey that brought me to Jesus and the gifts of truth and hope He has given me.

I am an old man now, for although I was young and strong when I began my journey, nearly forty years have passed. Yet, the memories of those great events are as fresh to me now as if they happened only yesterday.

First, I must tell you about myself. You have called me a "King of the Orient," and a "Wiseman" in your stories and songs. I was among those called Magi. I am from the Persian Empire, far to the east of Israel. My work was that of a teacher and instructor to the kings. I also performed an important role in the sacrifices in our temples, for no religious sacrifices were allowed in our land without one of the Magi present. We were skilled in philosophy, medicine, natural science, and the study of the stars. We worshipped fire and nature, thinking that in the worship of nature we would find the answers to life. Mostly, however, I was a man who sought the truth.

My king and all those in my country respected me. I had accumulated all a person could possibly want when it came to material riches. I had it all. . .or so I thought at first. Yet the more I gained the more empty I felt. Although I had much, my heart was empty.

I was a seeker for truth, looking for the hope that life held more than any possession. Political power could not bring inner peace. Wealth could not buy fulfillment for my soul. Religion and ritual could not cleanse my heart from the guilt of my sins. None of these things had

filled the void within me. . .

I must hasten on to tell you how our great adventure began. We studied the paths of the stars and planets. For us they represented the unchanging order of the universe. The stars, we believed, could be trusted to give direction and meaning to life. Many of us even believed a person's destiny was determined by the star under which they were born. Today you call this astrology. I have come now to realize that true guidance comes from the One who made the stars, but at the time I did not realize the truth. So we studied the stars, hoping to find truth and answers for our lives.

One particular night brought an extraordinary occurrence. A star we had not seen before appeared in the sky. It was so brilliant it immediately demanded our attention. The unchanging order of the skies had been broken! We knew the appearance of such a star must be a signal of something very significant. It was as if God Himself was breaking into His universe to tell the world something special.

Two of my friends became especially interested in that star with me. We began to search for its meaning.

Melchior was the oldest. He was a quiet man, thin, with a long gray beard. Melchior was a man to study something very thoroughly before he would choose to accept or believe in it.

Balthasar was middle-aged, more burly and impulsive than either of us. He was a man of action. Bright brown eyes sparkled behind his thick, dark beard.

I, Caspar, was the youngest. At the time, I had not yet grown a full beard. People said I had the fresh face of youth. I was always the most inquisitive of the Magi. I did not tell my friends of my hunger to find hope and truth, but I persuaded Melchior and Balthasar to help me study the star. Secretly I longed for the star to guide me, to give me the answers for my heart. Could it be this star was God's gift of hope for me? I did not know, but I was determined to discover its true meaning for myself.

So we studied the Star. We knew it was a special sign, but for what reason? Diligently we studied the events going on in the world. What we found made our curiosity greater and our eagerness to discover the secret of the star more intense.

As we studied the writings of other peoples, we learned that all across the world there was an intense conviction with a corresponding expectation that a great leader would be born. From Him would come the possibility of peace for all the people of our world.

We found that the Romans were talking of ushering in a "golden age," looking for a "savior" to bring in that age. Far to the east, in the land of China, their philosopher Confucius had spoken hundreds of years ago of the coming of a deliverer. We saw a pattern developing.

In these sources and others, we found there was an expectation of a great King who would come out of the region of Judea from among the Jewish people. Our own writings quoted a prophet from the Jews foretelling the coming of their Messiah, their Anointed One from God who would come to set all people free.

As we studied the writings of the Jewish prophets, they spoke of a child who would be born of a virgin. He would be a light to the world, a Wonderful Counselor, Mighty God, Everlasting Father, Prince of Peace.

All the sources pointed to the idea that God had given a special sign to announce that coming of a great King. As we charted the star, we saw that it had risen right over Judea.

There, indeed, a great King was to be born!

Looking back now, I can see that it was a wondering world that awaited the great King. There were cries of "peace, peace," but there was no peace. There was no joy nor peace in human hearts. Stress, worry, and anger ruled the hearts of most people, regardless of their language or country.

It was also a waiting world. People were looking for hope. They had discovered they could not build their "golden age" by themselves. They needed God and wanted Him to come to them.

I had a deep sense God was sending His answer to the world through this King.

So. . .now we understood what the Star was announcing to us! But what could we do? As we talked, Balthasar grew increasingly excited. He declared we should follow the star so we could see this King with our own eyes. I was only too pleased to follow the Star. Melchior hesitated briefly, but finally his excitement overcame his reluctance. We began to make preparations for the trip. Soon our caravan was ready, and we began our journey to the land of Judea, far to our west.

It was not an easy trip. We traveled rough trails with blistering hot days often followed by frigid bone-chilling nights. The possibility of an attack by thieves always lurked in the shadows. Yet, the Star—so brilliant, white, and shining—remained our constant guide. We felt a sense of peace and protection from that Star. We felt as if we were being guided by God Himself to a very important meeting. It was indeed to become a life-changing experience for all of us. Even the animals seemed to sense the significance of our journey, and gave us few problems.

Finally, after many months of travel, we reached Jerusalem, the most important city in all of Judea, and asked where we might find He who was born King of the Jews.

The people we met there were most interesting. . . .

We met Herod, the king of that region. He had ruled for many years. We knew in our hearts immediately he was not the promised king. He was only a pretender king. He was just a man who tried to act like a god. We found him to be almost insanely suspicious of anyone threatening his kingdom and his personal sovereignty. Herod was not pleased at all to hear of a king born who was the rightful ruler of the land. He was afraid that this little child was going to interfere with his life, his place, his power. Behind his feigned politeness, we could tell he wanted to eliminate the true King.

Then we met the Chief Priests of their Temple. They were the religious leaders of the land. We thought certainly they would be thrilled to hear about their foretold Savior-King. It was their own writings that showed the new King was to be born in the little town of Bethlehem. . .only six short miles from Jerusalem. They really surprised us. . .they were completely indifferent!

When we asked if they would like to go see the King, they replied that they could not come.

They were late for an important debate. . . . Besides, they said, they had rituals to perform. Although they knew much about God with their heads, it seemed they had completely missed Him in their hearts. Here was the fulfillment to all their prophecies, the answer to all God's promises. . .and they had no time for Him!

Ah, I see many still like them. . .people who get too busy with life— personal responsibilities, politics, social issues, even religious duties. The affairs of life demand so much of their attention that knowing the King for themselves means little or nothing to them. Their own self-righteousness blinds them to the truth.

So, leaving Herod and the religious leaders behind, we set our eyes on the Star and traveled in its light until it stopped right over the place where the Child King was staying.

We rejoiced with great joy. We were overwhelmed with wonder! The three of us clutched each other in our excitement. Here was the end of our journey at last. We had found the King!

Joseph and Mary, His parents, were not what we expected. They were but simple, common folk. The place where they were staying was poor. It was not the surroundings we had expected for a great King. There were no servants, no fanfare to announce our arrival.

With hesitant wonder, we went in to see the Person we had sought for so long. In the Child's presence we instinctively knew we were in the presence of royalty. When His parents told us His name, we were even more in awe. His name, they said, was Jesus. "Savior." Yes, this indeed was a special supernatural Child. This was God who had become a Man!

The three of us were used to being in the presence of kings, but this Child made me feel I was in the presence of the King of Kings. We knelt before this King and worshipped Him. How He would affect the whole world we did not know, but He had already captured my heart. For the first time, my heart felt like its long search for meaning was over.

We gave Him gifts. . .

Melchior gave Him gold, a gift for a King.

I, Caspar, gave Him frankincense, used in worship. It was a gift for a Priest. Somehow I knew this Child was to become the bridge between God and humanity.

Balthasar gave Him a gift that puzzled me then. He gave the Child the gift of myrrh, a spice used to prepare dead bodies for burial. None of us knew then what it would all mean, yet Balthasar said he felt he must give this Child this gift—a gift for one who was to die.

Even as I gave my gift to the new King, I felt He was giving me a gift as well. . .the gift of hope. I could look forward to my future because I had met the King. The light of the Star was now gone, but the Light of Hope was shining in my heart.

Our visit was much too short, but God warned us in a dream that we must not return to Jerusalem and report our findings to Herod. An angel of God told us to return home by a different route. And so we did.

After we returned to our own land, I did my best to keep track of the Child. I did not hear much for thirty years. The Child grew into a Man in a quiet village called Nazareth. Then I began to receive reports of how this Jesus did miracles that transformed people's lives. He taught powerful messages of life-changing truth even a child could understand. He spoke of hope and love, of forgiveness and peace with God. Peace with God brought the possibility of peace among human beings. His was a kingdom of love, not hate. Forgiveness, not fighting. Everywhere Jesus walked, people were never the same.

Then, the news came that Jesus had been crucified on a Cross. . .but He had risen from the dead only three days later! Balthasar's gift of myrrh made sense at last. This was a King born to die for His people, but even death could not overcome Him!

I realized then the gift Jesus had given the world—He gave His life so the sins separating us from God could be forgiven. We could have a personal relationship with the One who made the universe! The search for truth and meaning forever finds its culmination in the person of Jesus the Christ. His gift of love could bring peace to all who would receive it.

When I realized this, I knelt again in worship, this time to commit my life to Jesus, my King and my Savior. This time I gave Him the most important gift, really the only one I could give.

I gave Him my heart.

I pondered much the significance of the Star. As I studied further, I learned the Spirit of God sometimes reveals Himself as *Shekinah*—the glory of God Himself. I now believe the Star was the Spirit of God guiding us to find the Christ, providing light in our search through the darkness. He still does the same for every heart looking for truth.

I sought a Star, but found my Savior. In Him I found truth. . .hope. . .purpose. . .and so much more. Jesus changed my life! I know He can change yours as well if you choose. You can choose to reject Him like Herod. . .you can ignore Him as the religious leaders did. . .or you can join me and worship Him as King of your life.

I still find today what I learned then . . .

Wisemen still seek Him.

The Distance of Faith

The distance between religion and real faith is the span between the head and the heart. Annas had discarded that simple but essential truth a long time ago, but you'd never know by looking at him. Outwardly he wore all the trappings of a religious leader, the rich robe of a priest and an all-knowing expression. Inwardly there wasn't anything that resembled a real relationship with God. If you would have made that observation to Annas, however, he would have argued with you vehemently. He was, after all, one of the chief priests in Israel and a member of the prestigious Sanhedrin. To suggest that one could be a member of the highest religious ruling council in the land and not know God would be an insult.

Yet, in the inner recesses of his heart where only Annas and God could see, that was exactly Annas' spiritual condition. Dedicated to religion, devoid of a relationship with God.

Religion had always had its place in Annas' family. He grew up in a wealthy home with its material expectations, excesses, and entrance to exclusive places and positions. Their wealth also made it possible for Annas' father to be one of the Sadducees, an exclusive religious group made up of those with high social and financial standing. Religion, then, was something Annas had been born into as a social right.

It had, however, never been born into him as a relationship with God.

The Sadducees were one of three major religious groups that dominated the spiritual and political landscape of Israel. Each had its distinctions. Each tried to demote the others theologically and dominate them politically. Where the religion ended and the politics began was often impossible to tell. Both involved money. . .lots of it. One of the first lessons Annas had learned by observing his own father was: Money equals power. The more money, the more power.

The Sadducees rose to prominence in a time when Israel, as it had so often in the past, neglected to worship the Lord God Almighty and began to bow down instead to idols of gold. As people revered material wealth instead of the Maker of the Universe, the Sadducees, by virtue of their financial situation, gained more political standing. The appointment of Herod as king of their land by the Romans didn't hurt their power either. Real worship was far down their priority list, if on it at all.

Religious business, however, was right at the top of the list. One of the deals Herod cut with them was the rebuilding and expansion of the Temple. It became the pride of all Israel, especially the Sanhedrin. Herod built them their own special place on the Temple mount near the Temple itself to conduct their business. It was an awesome spectacle of architectural beauty.

A restored Temple meant renewed pride. It also meant renewed religious business as pilgrims came from all over to worship there. The Law required many sacrifices to keep spiritual accounts current with God. Consequently, many people brought offerings and purchased animals for sacrifice. The Sanhedrin developed a special Temple monetary system, mandating the exchange of all other forms of money for "Temple" money. At an exchange rate that left repentant pilgrims also empty in their pockets, it brought huge financial gains into Temple treasuries. The Sadducees oversaw a religious and financial empire driven by greed and power.

Things had not always been that way, however. Once the Sadducees saw themselves as the guardians of the written law and religious rituals. They oversaw the Scribes, whose jobs were to accurately record everything from the sacred writings to the daily proceedings of the king. To maintain order, they felt they needed to maintain tradition. They received a great deal of training in the Law and history of Moses and could recite sacred passages at great length. They did not, however, believe in the supernatural side of their religion. Resurrection from the dead and the existence of angels did not fit into their theological system. With their accumulated wealth, they didn't need supernatural wonders.

They were at odds with the Pharisees, the other prominent religious group besides the Scribes. The Pharisees were made up mostly of middle-class businessmen. Their distinction was their determination to be righteous through obeying religious laws and their dedication to oral traditions. Where the Sadducees honored the written law, the Pharisees had gone beyond the written law with commentaries and interpretations. Their oral traditions were passed on from generation to

generation, describing in minute detail how a person was to live out the Law in every conceivable area of life. They saw righteousness as a result of self-effort, not trust in God.

Both Sadducees and Pharisees still honored the Temple rituals, but the two groups spent extraordinary amounts of time pointing out their differences. Both felt they were protecting tradition and pleasing the Almighty, but it was obvious even to the Romans that God could leave and their systems would never know the difference.

Who needed God to give them power to live a holy life when they had all the rules for external righteousness already spelled out for them?

Who needed God when they could pride themselves in such a magnificent building?

Who needed God when adherence to religious regulations was more important than a pure heart?

Who needed the wonder of knowing an infinite God when scholars had written down all there was to know about Him?

Who needed God when you didn't believe in life after death and resisting Herod could mean certain physical expiration?

Annas had answered those questions in his own heart and decided God was important only toward the accumulation of political power and money. He cloaked himself with a religious veneer of wealth, social prestige, and political standing. His coveted goal was to become High Priest, the

ultimate position he could attain politically and religiously. He knew how to use his carefully crafted veneer to its full advantage in playing the cardinal games that would take him to the top.

The arrogance and hypocrisy God saw under the veneer made Him sick.

Worshipping God was not essential when getting along with Herod was expedient. Day by day, month by month, year by year, life in Israel continued as Annas and the rest of the Sanhedrin adhered to a dead form of religion without ever tasting the life and power of God. They never even knew what they were missing.

One day, however, visitors came from a distant country that completely upset their well-ordered rhythm of life. The visitors arrived at the palace of Herod requesting information about the whereabouts of the newborn King of Israel. They were looking for the One the Jewish Scriptures called the Messiah. Something inside Annas quivered when he heard the news.

The Messiah? No. . .it couldn't be. He knew the prophecies by heart, but he had dismissed them as irrelevant history. Annas had no room for Someone who might mess up all his plans. He was too close to moving into the coveted position of High Priest. If the Messiah was who they said He would be. . .then Messiah would properly take the God-ordained positions of prophet, king, . . . and priest. He would take the place Annas secretly cherished for himself. He had done well without this Messiah; even if He was from God, Annas didn't want Him. There was no room for God in his neatly ordered religious system.

Annas was surprised by these visitors. They were Magi, men holding positions very similar to his own in their native land. They too were respected in royal circles. They too were guardians of sacred things. They too wielded political influence. Outwardly, at least, Annas was looking into a proverbial mirror.

As the Magi told their story, however, he soon discovered that these men from the East were much different from himself. They had seen a brilliant Star, of supernatural origins they believed, appear in the heavens. One of them, Caspar by name, told of his hunger for truth that would bring inner fulfillment.

When the Magi finished the story of their incredible journey, Herod turned his attention to Annas and the other members of the Sanhedrin. "Where is this One to be born who would be called the King of the Jews?" Herod's voice was velvet soft, but it carried a distinct undertone of violence. Motioning to Annas to step forward, Herod awaited the response.

Time seemed to stand still for Annas. He knew the answer. Anyone with knowledge of the Scripture knew the Messiah would be born in Bethlehem, only six miles from Jerusalem. Micah had clearly proclaimed it hundreds of years ago. No, it would not be hard to recite from memory the answer to Herod's question. Bethlehem was the place to find the newborn King. What would be hard would be the answer to this question: What place would this Messiah have in Annas' heart?

Going with the Magi to worship this Messiah would mean risking Herod's wrath. It would also mean giving up all his carefully made plans for financial gain and political power. It would topple his neatly constructed religious system with Annas seated at the top. In short, this Messiah meant losing everything for which Annas had worked. . .and gaining everything for which God had created His nation. Annas inwardly groaned at the implications. This was one question he didn't want to answer.

"Well?" Herod's brusque inquiry snapped Annas back to attention. The Magi's eyes were bright with eagerness. Annas found he had been holding his breath.

He let it out slowly, then inhaled again. He had to answer. He couldn't risk displeasing Herod. In that same moment Annas also knew he could not risk the Messiah replacing his plans with His own rule.

"Bethlehem. . .the prophet Micah foretold the Messiah is to be born in Bethlehem." There. It was out. The Magi quickly begged the indulgence of Herod so they could travel the final miles of their quest to find the King. When Herod asked the Magi to bring back word of this newborn King so he might go worship also, Annas knew he dared not travel with them. If he did, Herod would probably make sure the six miles to Bethlehem were Annas' final miles. Ever.

All the other chief priests and scribes came to the same conclusion as Annas. They knew the fate of the Baby would be their fate if they didn't distance themselves from Him as quickly as possible. Politely declining the invitation of the Magi to accompany them to Bethlehem on the pretext of a scheduled debate at the Sanhedrin, Annas and the rest left quickly. They realized their condition would be tied to that of the Child. The stories of butchered babies in Bethlehem bore that out days later.

Caspar caught Annas' eye as he turned to go, and unwillingly Annas felt ashamed. As long as he lived, he would never forget the look of invitation and confusion Caspar gave him, no matter how much he tried. Of all the people who should have eagerly received news of their long-awaited Messiah, who should have joyfully joined a procession to worship Him, it should have been someone like Annas. He was a religious leader for his people. He was the guardian of the very Scriptures that pointed to the Messiah. His heart should have been the first to welcome the Messiah as Savior and rightful King. He should have been the first to proclaim to Israel's families that their Deliverer had arrived at last. Of all the responsibilities of a Chief Priest, this should have been his supreme opportunity. Caspar said nothing, but his puzzled look said everything.

Instead, Annas squelched the conviction tugging at his heart. He remained silent about the possibility that God's promises were gloriously true and available to all. He separated himself from any possibility of actually meeting the Messiah. His head had plenty of room for his religion. His heart had no room for his Messiah.

Time went on and things worked out as Annas planned. Herod, he thought, had dealt with the baby Messiah. Annas maneuvered his way into the position of High Priest and made sure relatives of his held the post for decades to follow. In fact, nearly thirty years later his son-in-law Caiaphas was elevated to High Priest while Annas ran things from behind the scenes. All he had planned for came to pass.

His religious empire seemed to be running smoothly until one day stories began to come from Galilee of a simple Carpenter who was doing miracles and teaching with supernatural authority. Some people were calling Him a prophet. Many were calling Him the Son of God.

When Annas heard that, he quivered inside the same way he had when he heard Caspar speak of the Messiah many years before. No. . .it couldn't be. Herod had taken care of Him. Yet the more Annas heard of Jesus of Nazareth the more he knew the Person he'd tried to ignore so long ago was confronting his heart again.

This time Annas didn't rely on a Herod. Using the political skills he'd honed over time, Annas orchestrated the death of Jesus, looking on in approval as a rabid crowd shouted to Pilate, "Crucify Him! His blood be upon us and our children!"

Twice Jesus sought entrance to Annas' heart, once as a newborn King and once as the Son of God. Twice Annas responded by seeking the death of Jesus. Twice by his own choice he called down the consequences of rejecting Jesus. The blood of Jesus was on his head.

There are still many like Annas today. For an Annas, religion is dominated by talk of buildings, doctrine, dollars, or position. Religious rituals, social issues, or political influence have long since diluted the good news of a Savior into tepid temporal words with no supernatural saving power. There is no room for a King from Heaven when there are so many pressing issues to deal with here on earth. After all, who needs God when we are taking care of His business so well on earth? In fact, a Savior convicting of sin and offering salvation for the heart would disrupt carefully guarded religious tradition and organization. Annas thought so. So do many with the same spiritual condition who sit in church buildings and in positions of religious leadership today. Dedicated to religion. Devoid of any relationship with God.

Yes, the distance between religion and real faith is the eighteen-inch span between the head and the heart.

It's also the distance between heaven and hell.

The Quiet Ones

Some people see God when no one else can.

They are often the quiet ones, unnoticed on earth but famous in heaven. While the more flamboyant are figuring out new ways to get people to listen to them, the quiet ones are finding new places to listen to God. While the impatient demand their way immediately, the waiters allow God to bring His best in His time. God delights in taking the quiet ones into His confidence. The Almighty chose to share His greatest secret with two of His patient waiters.

They were old. They had little money and even less influence. The movers, shakers, and power brokers of the Temple never even gave Anna or Simeon a second glance as they hurried from one important meeting to another. Heaven, however, leaned in to listen lovingly to their every prayer.

Anna's name meant "grace." She grew up in a home where worship was as natural as breathing. Her parents gave her a love for God's Word and God's house by the obvious way they lived out their love for Him. Even as a young girl Anna could tell when God was whispering special things to her heart. The Spirit of God found in her a heart that loved His companionship. He found far too few like her. The Spirit delighted in filling her open heart, molding it to reflect her name.

Anna married young. Seeing her husband as a gift from God, every morning for seven years she thanked the Lord for her life companion as she woke up next to him. Like every other young wife in her land, she dreamed of being the mother of the Messiah. Pouring out her love for the Lord and praying for her people continued as a natural rhythm in her life. The Spirit delighted in her prayers and let her know it by pouring His love back into her life. It overflowed easily and noticeably to others. Life was good for Anna.

In the seventh year of her marriage, her dream of a lifetime of love with her mate died when she made the painful transition from wife to widow. In the difficult months of sorrow that followed, she faced decisions that would determine her state of heart for the rest of her life. She could let her grief harden into bitterness. She could blame God for her loss and walk away from Him. She could recognize instead how the curse of sin is indiscriminate when it chooses its victims. She could look for another husband and risk the consequences of marrying on the rebound of bereavement. Anna's options were many. Swirling emotions could have led her down several paths. The advice she received, both invited and uninvited, was as varied as the number of her self-appointed counselors.

During her season of sorrow, the Spirit held her close to His heart, loving her through her pain, reassuring her that He would never leave her. As the ache of her grief was immersed in God's peace, she knew that of all the options presented to her, only one was right. Anna decided her only option was to choose God's option for her life. Instead of blaming God for taking away her gift, she chose to give her heart to the Giver as the Love of her life. It was a decision she never regretted.

Her singleness led her into a new season of life. She emerged from her season of sorrow deepened, sweetened, and even more dependent on the Spirit who so lovingly took care of her. She found herself drawn to pray as never before, finding a level of intimacy with God beyond any human relationship she had ever known.

The Spirit began to trust her with special messages to give to others. As always, she never called attention to herself, but people who hungered to hear from God often found themselves led to her. For many, listening to Anna pray was a rich experience they remembered long after being with her. They noticed in her an intimacy with the Almighty lacking in most of the professional priests. Anna didn't need applause or affirmation from others, she didn't have a position to protect and was oblivious to religious political games. She simply delighted in pointing people to the Lord she loved so much. Just being with Anna made people want to spend more time with God. Many also left a visit with her with a word from God that specifically and directly applied to a situation no one else knew about. Each time she passed along a message from the Spirit, she felt His smile. That was all the approval Anna ever needed.

Over the years, Anna continued to minister in her quiet powerful way. Decades passed. Some said she was in her eighties; others thought she had been a widow for over eighty years. Age had ceased to matter for her. Her body showed the outward effects of accumulated decades of time, but her smile sparkled with the timeless love in her heart. She continued to pray. She listened to the voice of the Spirit and shared His heart with others as He set up divine appointments for her.

Her hunger for God to move in her nation intensified, and she found herself spending most of her time in the Temple Court of the Women worshipping. . .fasting. . .praying. . .listening. Anna's prayers were sweet music in Heaven. The Spirit spoke quietly to her, letting her know that her time on earth would not be complete until she visibly saw His greatest gift to her and to her people.

Close by in the Court of the Men was another of God's waiters. He too was old and had known his share of sorrows during the course of his life. Simeon, whose name meant "listening," was known for his complete devotion and holy lifestyle. Simeon not only listened to the Holy Spirit, he lived out what he heard. Here too the Spirit found a yielded heart all too rare among His people. Simeon also spent much time praying for his people over the course of many years. He too knew the distinct and unique experience of recognizing the voice of God speaking to him. It was a privilege he never took lightly and he experienced it often.

There came a day when the Spirit spoke so vividly and clearly to Simeon that His words became indelibly etched on the old man's spirit. Simeon was praying, as he often did, for "the Consolation of Israel," a common term used to describe God's promised Messiah. Some scoffed at him for even praying like that. After all, there had been no miracle or revelation from God for over four centuries. Religion flowing from the reality of a relationship with a living God had steadily deteriorated into a dead system of rules, rituals, and religious politics. The system was corrupt, God was silent, and the Scriptural promise of a Savior no longer inspired many people. Few could contradict Simeon's integrity, but most could not understand the quality of his spirituality.

In this context Simeon continued to pray, ignoring his detractors. He knew others still prayed as he did. The Spirit made sure His quiet ones knew about each other. Although it was not considered proper for men and women to converse in the Temple courts, Anna and Simeon had a Spirit-initiated connection that led them to quietly encourage each other as faithful listeners to the Spirit's voice.

On that special day, Simeon had been praying as he usually did. Everything seemed ordinary, until his heart sensed the unique stirring when the Spirit had something distinct to share with him. He could never really describe the feeling, because the experience was deeper than an emotion. When the Spirit spoke He did so on a heart-to-heart basis.

Simeon. . .the Spirit's voice was quiet but clear.

Yes, Lord? came his humble, oft-used response. *Your servant is listening. . .*

Simeon. . .I have heard your prayers for Messiah to come. I am pleased with them. You have wondered why you are still here on earth even though you are so old. I know you long to join your loved ones here with Me, but I have kept you alive for a special purpose. Simeon. . .your own eyes will look upon your Messiah. I want you to announce My blessing on Him when His parents bring Him to the Temple for His dedication.

Simeon's eyes opened wide as he tried to grasp the Spirit's words. Him? An old man most people had long since stopped noticing? Why should he be so honored among all the men of the nation? He didn't question the Spirit's assignment. . .he just could not immediately comprehend it. What he did understand, he embraced. What he couldn't comprehend, he entrusted to the Spirit.

Yes, Lord. . .it would be my great honor. Simeon's unspoken words were sweet music in the Spirit's ears. In his heart, Simeon felt the warmth of the Spirit's smile. For him, too, that smile was all the approval necessary.

Simeon expected the special message to precede its fulfillment by only a short period of time. Surely he would recognize the Messiah in just a matter of days, or perhaps weeks! Each time he entered the Temple he took particular notice of all new parents presenting their children for dedication. He continued to listen for the Spirit's nudge. . . .

The dedication of children was a sacred occasion in Israel. Boys were circumcised on the eighth day with the intimate identifying mark of being one of God's chosen people. Later the child's parents were required to bring the child with an offering to "redeem" the child from God. Those financially well-off brought a lamb for sacrifice. Poor parents were allowed to bring two young pigeons. The ceremony was a continual reminder that every child was a gift from God. Parents brought their baby to figuratively return the gift of a child back to the Lord.

The ceremony was also a commitment by the parents to live in such a way that their son or daughter would find it easy to dedicate their lives to God when they could choose for themselves. Ceremonial dedication of children took place daily in the presence of a rabbi, friends, and family. Only the Lord Himself knew the true depth of the parents' consecration at that moment. Time would make visible their true priorities to everyone.

God's timing, however, was not Simeon's. Days became weeks. Weeks turned into months. Months stretched into years. Simeon watched diligently, yearning for the moment the Spirit would speak the identifying word. Through it all he kept praying expectantly. Few knew of his special assignment. Anna knew. Together they waited.

It was an early spring day when Simeon sensed the unique inner stirring of the Spirit's Presence. Something important was about to happen. His heart began to beat faster in anticipation. His spirit seemed to lean forward to listen intently for what the Spirit was about to say. Somehow he knew his years of waiting and listening were about to be over.

Simeon. . .He knew that Voice so well!

Yes, Lord? The stirring inside was so strong he was trembling.

Simeon. . .today is the day. Go to the Temple. Watch. Today your eyes will look upon your Messiah. The Spirit was enjoying this immensely.

Yes, Lord! The joy of an old listener and the Eternal Spirit blended together. Simeon's joy flowed from a heart whose anticipation was about to be fulfilled. The Spirit's joy flowed from His pleasure in a faithful man. Suddenly Simeon felt as if God Himself was taking his hand. Together they walked out, hand in hand, toward the Temple.

Anna was in her customary place of prayer in the Temple when her heart also heard the familiar stirring of the Spirit. Instinctively she held her breath as she listened. The Spirit spoke. Another waiter eagerly anticipated a divine appointment she had prepared for her whole life.

When Simeon arrived, still hand in hand with the Spirit, his heart raced and his face glowed in anticipation. As soon as he entered the Temple gates, Anna knew Simeon was there even though she couldn't see him.

It would not be long now.

Simeon positioned himself so he could see every baby arriving in the arms of his parents. What would the parents of the Messiah look like? A couple, obviously wealthy, walked by with their newborn son. Their sacrifice of a lamb meant they were people of means. Them? No. Another husband and wife, members of a priestly family, entered with a baby boy. Perhaps from a line of spiritual leaders. . . Still nothing from the Spirit.

Through the door of the Temple court came a young couple. The mother, barely a teenager, lovingly held an infant boy. The husband carried two small pigeons in hands rough from long hours of hard labor. It was obvious they were not wealthy. No one seemed to notice them in the crowd. . . .

Suddenly Simeon's spirit leaped to attention. This unlikely couple? They were poor. They were simple, humble, nondescript people like so many. . . .

Simeon. . .

Them, Lord?

Yes. . .go behold your Messiah. Not far away, Anna was hearing the same words.

The old man wobbled in trembling excitement as he wove his way through the crowd to the young couple. He stopped in front of them, speechless, his sparkling eyes speaking volumes.

Joseph and Mary looked into the face of an old man they had never met, but the expression on his face they had seen before—in the faces of shepherds retelling a story of angelic announcements in wonder-filled amazement. . .

in the faces of Zechariah and Elizabeth after their own son's miraculous birth. . .

and now in the face of this man.

He knew.

This old man standing before them with the glow of heaven on his face knew who they were! More importantly, he knew who their Son was. Once again, Joseph and Mary were humbled and overwhelmed by the protective care of their Heavenly Father. Then the Spirit whispered to them, and they knew who the old man was. A rabbi would perform a ceremony without a clue as to what he was actually doing, but this old man of God would pronounce God's blessing and

know exactly who he was blessing. Simeon was God's choice for this sacred moment.

Joseph turned to Mary. The look that passed between them said it all. Without a word, Mary gently put Jesus into the arms of Simeon. The old man who had waited and listened so long was holding the dream of his heart and the Deliverer of the world in his arms at last.

For a long moment, all he could do was gaze into the infant's face. He was much too full of wonder for words to come. . .so full he ached with the joy pushing open every door in his heart. This Baby. . .the Consolation of Israel. The Messiah. . .snuggled close to his heart! Jesus looked into the wrinkled tearstained face of the old listener, smiled, and reached up to give Simeon's beard a baby tug. Joseph, his arm around Mary, couldn't help but give a proud father's laugh at the sight. Mary stood, eyes glistening, her heart recording every moment. Meanwhile, the Spirit had taken Anna by the hand and was leading her to the three faithful hearts and a Baby.

Simeon brought Jesus near until his bearded cheek nestled the Baby's soft infant cheek. What do you say when God has given you the desire of your heart after years of faithful waiting? Looking up, tears of joy still streaming down his face until they were captured by his beard, Simeon's heart overflowed in worship:

"Sovereign Lord, You can now release Your servant in peace as You promised. With my own eyes You have allowed me to see Your salvation; it's now out in the open for everyone to see! Here is Your Light to reveal Yourself to the Gentiles. . .here is the One who will reveal Your glory to Your people Israel."

Mary and Joseph stood speechless in wonder at Simeon's words. Still holding Jesus, Simeon reached over and put his hand in blessing on Joseph's head, then on Mary's. As his hand rested on Mary, the Spirit whispered something to him. The words thrilled and pained him at the same time. He knew the words were for Mary, so he told her the Spirit's message. As he spoke, he had the look of a man seeing ahead down the corridors of time:

"This Child's destiny is to bring about the failure and recovery of many in Israel. He will be misunderstood and resented because He will reveal people's hearts for what they really are in God's sight. They will reject Him. . ." Simeon paused and looked at Mary with deep compassion. "And when they do, the pain of a sword will pierce your heart, too."

Joseph instinctively held Mary closer, and Simeon's hand seemed to rest protectively on her head. Mary, her eyes wide, nodded slowly. More than thirty years later, those words would come back to her as she stood in front of a Cross. . .her Son's Cross.

Anna had come up to them as Simeon's prophetic words began to flow from his heart. Not wanting to disturb the divine moment, she waited until he was finished and then moved to Simeon's side, her face glowing with the same glory Simeon's face radiated. Mary and Joseph looked into

Anna's face, then again at each other.

This old listener knew, too.

Simeon looked down at Anna. Neither spoke, but the two who had waited until the very end of their lives to see the fulfillment of their dreams knew the wait had been worth it. The two aged quiet ones stood with the young parents and their Baby in the middle of the crowded Temple court. Few noticed what took place in that sacred moment there. Few had hearts tuned to the Voice of the Spirit. Few had eyes open to see God when He was right there in front of them.

Only the quiet ones knew. The listeners. The waiters. The ones who let God set the agenda, the time, and the place of their miracle.

Looking down on Mary, Joseph, Anna, and Simeon, the Spirit smiled on them. They basked in the warmth of that familiar Smile.

As it had always been, that Smile was all they needed.

Threat to the Throne

When he leaned forward, we saw insanity in his eyes.

"What did you say about a newborn king?" Herod's voice was so low it almost purred, but his tone carried an undercurrent of death. The jewels on his crown sparkled as an insignia of royalty, but the glitter in his eyes signaled mental instability. Something inside me suddenly felt sick. This was not the response these Magi expected in their quest to worship a new king. . .not at all. After following a Star hundreds of miles and dozens of days under divine inspiration, they anticipated delighted celebration. Instead they found themselves looking into the face of poorly disguised desperation. Instinctively they knew the baby they came to exalt was on a short list to become extinct.

What they felt instinctively I knew was reality.

For Melchior, Balthasar, and Caspar, coming to the opulent palace of Herod in Jerusalem was the obvious place to find the newborn king they had traveled so far to worship. Jerusalem was the capital. Herod was the king. Herod was almost seventy. . .far past the life expectancy of people in this part of the world, even rich people. Herod would be planning for a son of his to take over his throne. A delegation of visitors from a great distance to help celebrate the advent of a new king's reign should have been a tremendous compliment to his reputation. But the response they were getting was just the opposite of what they would have predicted. What was going on here? This didn't make sense.

It made perfect sense to me, however, because I'd seen this all before.

There was more going on here than they could have realized. What the three Magi couldn't see was the turmoil of jealousy swirling in Herod's heart. What they didn't know was his deadly history of guarding his personal sovereignty, Herod's lifelong internal battle to be in control of his world. The casualties of his conflict were numerous. . .with lethal consequences to anyone he saw as a threat to his throne.

I'd been watching Herod's internal struggle for decades now. . .and I was probably the only one still alive who had known him that long. I was Herod's cupbearer, his confidant, and the closest thing Herod ever had to a friend. Many years ago, I had met Herod when we were both young men. For some reason I've never been able to understand, Herod took a liking to me and decided I was someone he could trust. Perhaps it was my name, Hermes, which means "good luck." Perhaps it was something else that Herod saw in me. . .I'll never know. At any rate, Herod decided he needed someone he could trust with his life, and I was that person. I'd been with him through his years of ascent to political influence. I had also seen over those years his descent into madness and suspicion. As Herod's cupbearer, it was my responsibility to taste everything before Herod ate or drank in order to protect him from being poisoned. Herod knew in some way his life was in my hands. I think that's what kept me alive all those years I lived so close to a man who wound up destroying everyone he allowed to come close to him.

Watching Herod's life from up close had been like looking at a puzzle within a paradox. Long ago Herod had sold his soul for the promise of power. Born half-Jew and half-Idumaen, he had the blood of two rival nations flowing in his veins. Not feeling accepted by either ethnic side of his heritage, he decided to play both sides to his personal advantage. His need for acceptance soon manifested itself in a driving obsession for power. He would make people need him. . .and they'd have to accept him whether they wanted to or not! As with most who live from a shaky base of insecurity, Herod sought to keep things under his control with ruthless abuse of authority. I saw in Herod an inner need for a healthy identity struggling with a sense of insecurity. Over time, this became insanity protecting a warped sense of personal sovereignty.

Over forty years had passed since he aligned himself with the Roman rulers of his native Israel. It was about that time forty years ago "chance" made our paths to cross, and our unlikely "friendship" started. A young man of about twenty-five then, he realized his path to power was to make himself useful to those who currently held it. . .and the Roman road was his path. Through flattery, political intrigue, and the timeless art of bribery, he got himself appointed as governor over Israel. Seven years later he took the title of king of the Jews. Rome supplied the resources. Herod reveled in the appearance of royalty. I enjoyed being along for the ride.

Being of mixed bloodlines, he was labeled unfit to rule by religious leaders who traced their pure priestly lineage back hundreds of years. No half-Jew, especially one who was a political puppet of the hated Romans, was suited to be their king. Only a man with the royal blood of King David's line flowing his veins could truly rule the people of Israel. Herod realized the members of the Sanhedrin, the nation's ruling religious body, would be nothing but problems because of their tremendous influence. His solution to the bloodline problem was to spill Sanhedrin blood. He had many of them executed and replaced with "religious" people more in line with his viewpoints. After all, no one was going to tell him what to do. . .especially not some narrow-minded bigots who called him to accountability in the name of God! Herod outwardly knew how to bow to appease Roman emperors, but inwardly he bowed to no one. He was not just king of the Jews…he was his own little god. The universe revolved around his throne. Any challenge to his power was a threat to his godhood. Herod behaved as he pleased without restraint. He sovereignly decreed a judgment of death on any and all who even hinted at hindering him.

I found myself taking care of a man who could act like an autocratic tyrant in public and cower like a haunted, insecure little boy in private. Few people knew the Herod I did. I guess my sense of pity and a warped sense of loyalty kept me at his side. Even if few loved him, I could see Herod was determined that no one would ever forget him.

To that end, he decided to leave many monuments to himself. He built magnificent theaters, amphitheaters, and racecourses to stage cultural events and athletic games in honor of Caesar. Entire cities were restored and improved, including a cosmopolitan jewel by the Mediterranean Sea he renamed Caesarea, again to keep him in Rome's good graces. Military fortresses and Gentile temples were erected all over the land. Several palaces, including the impregnable Masada, dotted Israel, all

devoted to display his splendor. He filled them with great thinkers and men of cultural accomplishments, hoping to elevate his reputation by being in the company of people of high standing.

His ultimate architectural achievements, however, were in Jerusalem itself. His fortress of Antonia was a gilded reminder to all of his golden rule…he had the gold, so he made the rules. Yet, strangely, Herod's unfulfilled obsession to be accepted sometimes showed itself in generosity. A few times when poor harvests made life extremely difficult for the common people, he reduced their taxes to ease the burden. Once, during a time of intense famine, he actually melted down some of his gold plate to buy corn for the starving people. The same man who could summarily execute their religious, political, and business leaders could also buy the common folk food in time of need. It seemed to me that perhaps Herod had some unspoken need to atone for his atrocities. No one really knew. I did know from the reports I received that his erratic behavior made him even more a feared enigma to the people of Israel.

His greatest building by far, only steps away from Antonia, was the Temple he rebuilt in Jerusalem. Religious leaders declared "he who has never seen the Temple of Herod has never seen a beautiful building." The description also revealed its inherent flaw. It was Herod's Temple, not God's. Herod had it built to appease the political appetites of the religious insiders and the religious appetites of the people, but his intent was to make sure people remembered him as its builder. God was just a convenient part of the equation to keep his throne and place in history secure.

His attempts to make a name for himself went beyond his material accomplishments. He married ten times, each time mainly to strengthen his political position. His inability to love and his infamous jealousy made his relationships with his wives and children a sordid mess. Tales from the Herodian palace made for delicious gossip both in Israel and Rome. As the number of his wives, children, and years increased, so did his insane jealousy. Rivals to his throne, real or perceived, were summarily dealt with by assassination. Not even his own family was safe from his suspicions. First came the murder of his wife Mariamne, whom he suspected of being unfaithful. Next came the execution of Mariamne's mother, Alexandra, who attempted to position one of her grandsons to take Herod's place on the throne. Over the course of time Herod ordered the assassinations of his sons Antipater, Alexander, and Aristobulus as well as other men with relational claims to the throne. Herod's reputation for political murder was so atrocious that at one point the Roman emperor Augustus bitterly remarked that it was safer to be Herod's pig than his son. Part of me was appalled by Herod's murderous decisions…and part of me tried to keep him appeased so I could stay alive.

All these horrific activities, of course, only made Herod all the more feared and reviled by the people he ruled. Knowing that made him even more determined to impress himself on the people. As he neared seventy and his physical health began to deteriorate (everyone knew his mental health had long since disintegrated, a fact I had been trying to keep hidden for years), he made one last desperate attempt to be remembered. Retiring to Jericho, the most naturally beautiful of all his cities, he ordered a large number of the most prominent and distinguished citizens of Jerusalem arrested on trumped-up charges. Keeping them imprisoned, he decreed that at the moment of his death, they too would all die. He knew no one would mourn his departure from this world, so he grimly insured tears would be shed at his death. Because he thought he was on the throne at the center of his universe he was willing to go to any extreme to stay there. Herod was carrying his obsession to the most deadly degree. He made me promise to carry out his death wish decree.

It was at that tragic and strategic moment the three Magi arrived in Jerusalem with their question about the location of the newborn King of the Jews. Hurrying back from Jericho, Herod called the visitors to appear before his throne. The thought of another possible rival to his reign infuriated and frightened him. Although I had seen this reaction too many times before, it still unnerved me.

All of Jerusalem shivered in fear of his inevitable reaction.

"Where is He who has been born King of the Jews? We saw His Star rise in the east, and we have followed it here. . .we have come to worship Him." At first the Magi's question made little sense, but as Herod interrogated them further, there appeared to be a supernatural element to their journey beyond his understanding. Quickly I summoned the chief priests and scribes at his command. When they arrived, he demanded an explanation as to where a political ruler with spiritual ramifications was supposed to be born.

To Herod's surprise, the answer was glibly given. It had been written down almost seven hundred years before by the prophet Micah, and the religious leaders recited it from memory:

"And you, Bethlehem, in the land of Judah are by no means least among the rulers of Judah; for from you shall come a ruler who will shepherd My people Israel."

There it was, in simplicity and clarity. God Himself was going to send a ruler, born in the city that claimed King David as its own. Bethlehem would birth Herod's rival.

He would make sure this child would not be his replacement.

I watched Herod's eyes narrow as he viewed the response of the two groups in front of him. The Magi received the news with eagerness. They asked the indulgence of the king so they could quickly finish their mission. The answer to their search was just six miles away! Ordering them to return with news of any child they might find fitting their description, he let them go. What we didn't know was his ill-disguised suspicion and a God-initiated vision would ensure the three Magi would never be back.

It was the utter indifference of the chief priests and scribes that stopped Herod from taking immediate action. They made no effort to accompany the Magi to Bethlehem. Why? If the birth of this child was the fulfillment of their messianic prophesies, wouldn't they be even more eager to bring him welcoming worship? Either they really didn't believe their sacred writings, or they were in fear of Herod's retaliation of anyone associated with a new king. Herod decided their indifference, for whatever reason, was reason enough for him to wait until more proof of a pretender king could be substantiated. I knew their "indifference" flowed out of their instinct for survival. As I had done so many times in the past, I too remained silent out of that same instinct.

When the Magi didn't return and rumors generated by shepherds telling stories of angelic visits started surfacing around Jerusalem, Herod decided he couldn't wait any longer to deal with this latest threat to his throne. Whether this child was actually sent by God or not really didn't matter. In fact, God was the ultimate threat to his personal sovereignty. God was the only one he couldn't eliminate by royal decree. . . or could he?

If this child represented both God and man, both the spiritual and political implications of this threat could be dealt with in one blow. Exterminate the child. . .eliminate the threat. The problem was. . .which child? The Magi had not revealed the date of his birth. Bethlehem, although not a large city, would certainly have a number of newborn boys. As I had many times in the past, I watched Herod's twisted mind begin to contrive a plan. . . .

That night soldiers burst into every Bethlehem home, swords drawn. Every boy under the age of two was roughly yanked from his mother's arms. The screams of startled infants were cut short by cold steel. Only the wailing of horrified parents continued into the darkness. The one baby Herod wanted to eliminate had escaped with His parents to Egypt. The King of the Universe placed Him under the protection of Heaven's finest warriors, untouchable to Herod's soldiers.

Once again, at least in his own mind, Herod's sovereignty was secure. He retired again to Jericho, confident of his place in history, yet still glaringly insecure about his identity. Not long after, however, he entered eternity. It was then that I knew all Herod's manipulations would no longer help him. The puny puppet king met the King of the Universe. The One rival to the rule of his universe he could not eliminate handed down Herod's final decree. Herod discovered the power of infinite sovereignty and divine justice. Herod's "reign" was over. The Baby of Bethlehem's reign will never end.

After living so close to Herod for so long, I've come to realize that flawed logic of the concept of personal sovereignty—no human is suited to take the place of deity. We do a woefully inadequate job of attempting to control our own little universe. Only God has the ultimate power over life and death, because the eternal destiny of every human being is in His hands. Whenever we try to take control of our little universe, we only wind up hurting others and ourselves. We mock the rightful rule of Almighty God in our lives. Our world disintegrates into a chaos we can't orchestrate even if we wear a cool outward facade of control.

I've also come to realize that "Herod" lives in all our hearts. We may never carry our outward actions to his extremes, but we continue his inward attitudes whenever we resist Jesus as our King. A battle continues to rage in every heart…who will rule? God will not share His rightful place as King with anyone. He can't. He's the only One Who deserves it. Consequently, either we have to yield our throne or try to make God yield His. Ultimately one will not survive.

It is only when we relinquish control of our life to Christ that the Herod in us dies. It is then life takes on supernatural dimensions beyond our human control, because God's sovereign plan for our lives is infinitely better than any we could ever attempt to engineer.

We all have to make that choice of who will be in control of our lives. Ultimately and eternally it means life or death. Will we make Christ King of our hearts? It's the one decision that makes all the difference for our destiny.

I watched Herod make his choice.

I've made mine.

What's yours?

Christmas Lamb

"Why, Father? Why are they hurting that man?" The tear-filled eyes looking up at Judah and the pleading tone of his little boy's voice shook him back to attention.

Father and son had been standing transfixed in stunned horror at the sight of three men hanging on rough blood-soaked crosses. It was the Man on the middle Cross that captured their attention. Some around them were openly sobbing, gasping through their tears that He had done nothing wrong. An innocent Man was dying in front of them. His little boy's confused question brought to his memory a question Judah had asked his own father decades earlier. . . .

Judah had shivered against the chill of the night air, snuggling closer to his father as they stood on the hillside overlooking the valley below. It was a clear winter night, and the stars were brilliant against the inky night sky. For a boy Judah's age, it was an honor just to be out in the fields shepherding the flock at night, so he didn't want his father to know he was cold. Nevertheless, the warm woolen garment his mother had made him could not keep the night chill from nipping at Judah's nose, fingers, and toes.

He shivered again. His father Isaac looked down at him with a twinkle in his eye. "It is cold out here, isn't it, Son?" he said quietly. "Do you want to go back with the others as they rest and get under one of the warm blankets? I can join you when my watch is up."

"No, Father, I want to stay with you!" Judah had been waiting for a long time to have the chance to stand night watch. Giving in to the cold now would remind him that he was still a boy when he wanted so much to be recognized as a young man. "Besides, I want to be out here with Mitzar, too."

His father looked at him fondly for a moment. "All right, Judah ben Isaac, my son so eager to be grown-up, I will allow you to stay here with me. But as for that lamb you have named Little One,

you'll have to let him sleep by his mother. You shouldn't get too attached to him, because he will not be sleeping out here in the fields with his mother too much longer."

Judah knew the answer before the words came out of his mouth, but he asked the question anyway. "Why, Father? Why?"

This was one of those moments that come between a father and son. . . a teachable moment that can influence the heart of the son for many years to come. Isaac was quiet for a moment, praying for the Lord to give him a simple yet wise answer to his son's request. What his son needed to know went far beyond the fate of one little lamb. His son's understanding of his own destiny could be affected by how he answered Judah's question.

"Judah. . .there is a simple answer to your question, but many things you need to understand go beyond my simple answer. The flock of sheep we watch over tonight is a very special flock. Here in the fields outside of Bethlehem, we are only a few miles from the Temple in Jerusalem. These sheep are destined to go to the Temple to be offered as sacrifices. Mitzar and all the other lambs are nearing the age when they must go to the Temple."

"And at the Temple they will sacrifice Mitzar?" Judah's small voice broke with the sorrow he felt at the thought of his Mitzar being killed. "But why, Father? Mitzar is just a little lamb. He is innocent. He has never done anything that would deserve such a fate."

Isaac's eyes grew moist as he saw the internal struggle going on in his son. "Yes, Judah, Mitzar will die at the Temple. Yes, he is an innocent lamb, but that is why Mitzar must die. The priests will take a knife, sacrifice him on the altar of the Lord, and his blood will pour out to cover our sins. It is the only way we can have God's forgiveness."

"But Father. . .such a terrible price to pay for one so innocent. Isn't there another way?"

"I wish there could be, my son. From the very beginning of time, God created all creatures and told us that 'the life is in the blood.' The blood represents the life of the creature. It was never God's desire for blood to be spilled out this way."

"What happened, Father? Why is it that one as innocent as Mitzar would have to have his blood poured out? Why would he have to die?"

"Something terrible happened, Judah. Something so terrible that it separated us from the God who made us and loves us. Something so terrible it required the awful price of countless lambs like Mitzar dying upon the altar of the Lord. That terrible thing happened when our first father and mother chose to reject God's good plan for their lives and rebel against His rightful place as Lord of their hearts. Sin came. . .and with it came death. Sin came like a deadly disease and it now infects every person."

"Is that what happened when Grandmother became sick last year before she died?" Judah's lip trembled as he thought about the lingering, anguishing death that had taken his beloved grandmother just months ago.

Pain haunted Isaac's eyes as he too remembered the trauma of losing his own mother. "When sin came into our world, my son, all of creation came under a curse. With that curse comes sicknesses like the one that took your grandmother from us. With that curse of sin comes all the evil that overflows out of men's and women's hearts. . .hatred, jealousy, bitterness, greed, anger, prejudice, selfishness, impurity. . .and many more sins I cannot mention to one as young as you are. With that curse of sin comes physical death. . .and also spiritual death. Sin separates us from our Holy God. It is a monstrous affront to His love. We have all sinned, Judah. . .we've all like sheep gone astray and gone our own way. By our own choices we have been cut off from knowing the God who loves us. . . and if we die in our sins, we will have chosen to be separated from Him forever. It is because God loves us so much that He has made a way for us to be forgiven and come close to Him again."

"What is that way, Father?" Judah's eyes were large as he looked up at his father's strong face.

"In order for the sins of the guilty to be forgiven, one who is innocent must die in their place.

The lifeblood of the guilty is tainted by their sin, so the lifeblood of one who is innocent covers the sins of the guilty. That is why every day, morning and evening, an innocent lamb like Mitzar is sacrificed at the Temple. It has been happening for hundreds of years, my son, and will continue until. . ."

"Until what, Father? Will there come a day when lambs like Mitzar will not have to be sacrificed for my sins and others?"

"Yes, there will be a day like that, Judah. It is a day we all have waited and longed for. . .a day when the cruel tyrant of sin is finally defeated once and for all. The prophet Isaiah heard the word of the Lord nearly seven hundred years ago, and he wrote:

"But, oh, how few believe it! Who will listen? To whom will God reveal His saving power? In God's eyes He was like a tender shoot, like a little lambkin, growing up in a world dry and barren. In our eyes, there was no attractiveness in Him at all. . .nothing to make us want Him. We despised and rejected Him. . .a man of sorrows, acquainted with bitterest grief. We turned our backs on Him and looked the other way as He went by. He was despised and we didn't care. Yet. . .it was our grief He bore. . .our sorrows that weighed Him down. And we thought His troubles were a punishment from God, for His own sins! But He was wounded and bruised for our sins. He was chastised that we might have peace. . .by the stripes He bore, we are healed and made whole! We are the ones who strayed away like sheep. We, who left God's paths to follow our own. Yet. . .God laid on Him the guilt and sins of every one of us.

"God Himself will provide a Lamb for the sins of all people. No matter how bad our sins may have been, God's Lamb—the Messiah—will become a perfect sacrifice for our forgiveness." He paused for a moment, thinking, then said, "Do you remember when our people left the land of Egypt?"

Judah nodded. He had heard the story of God's mighty deliverance of His people many times. It was one of the most important stories in their people's history.

"The night before God set His people free from the hand of Pharaoh, He sent the death angel in judgment across the land. He told His people to take a spotless lamb, to sacrifice it, and wipe its blood over the door of their homes. When the death angel saw the blood, he would pass over that home and all inside would be safe from death. Wherever the angel did not see the blood, the judgment of death for sin came to the firstborn of that home. That is why we still celebrate the Passover now. It was the blood of innocent lambs that saved our people then. It is the blood of countless innocent lambs that stands between our sins and God's judgment now. And. . .when God sends His Lamb, His blood will cover and wash away all the sins of those who will come to Him in faith. Without the blood, we have no hope."

Judah was quiet for a moment. "Is it really that bad, Father? Are people really so bad? Aren't there some sins that don't need God's forgiveness? Can't we just try hard to be better so God can accept us?"

Isaac knew that he was getting to the heart of what his son needed to know. If he missed this all-important lesson, his son would believe a lie that would cripple him spiritually. "Son, do you remember the night we put the sheep in the fenced pen, and in the morning we found that they had all gotten out? There was just one break in the fence, but it was enough for all the sheep to go astray. Sin is like that. . .it only takes one sin to stain our hearts and separate us from God. . . to lead us astray from Him. All sin is like this. . .whether we commit many or few, because all sin is choosing to go our own way instead of God's way. Yet, because of His mercy, God chooses to forgive all our sins because of the blood of the lamb and our humble confession. There is only one sin that God cannot forgive, however. . ."

"What would that be, Father?"

"The only sin God cannot forgive is the worst of them all. It is the sin of thinking we are so good in ourselves that we do not need God's forgiveness. . .when we lie to ourselves and try to make our sins not appear to be so bad. . .calling them mistakes instead of sins. It is the monstrous sin of telling God we are so good that we can be our own savior and god. . .when we will not acknowledge our need. . .when we reject His love and let our own pride separate us from Him. Some of the people who think they are the closest to God are actually the farthest away because they believe the lie of their own selfish pride and will not humble themselves before our Almighty Holy God. Because they will not come to God for forgiveness, He cannot forgive them. Do you understand, my son? Until you understand how horrible sin really is, you will not understand nor appreciate what an awesome thing the blood of the lamb really is."

In Judah's heart, the truth of his father's words broke through into his understanding. The innocent taking the place of the guilty. The black deadly poison of sin that would separate him from the God who loved him would require the lifeblood of his little Mitzar. The promise of God to send His own Son to be the sacrificial Lamb for the sins of every person. Tears began to run down Judah's face, and he noticed that his father's eyes were brimming with tears as well. "I understand, Father. Oh, how it hurts my heart, but I understand. Father. . .will God's Lamb come soon?"

"I don't know, my son. We can pray and ask, but God Himself will set the time when He sends His Messiah. . ."

Suddenly the night sky lit up with the bright light of a million candles. The suddenness of it knocked Judah and his father to the ground, and they could hear the startled cries of the other shepherds as they were awakened. Although the light was so bright it nearly blinded them, it was soft and somehow filled with peace. The air was charged with the electricity of supernatural presence. Hovering in the air above them, they saw an angel. . .and then behind him the sky was filled with angels like a mighty army.

For a moment they were too shaken to speak. Judah, wide-eyed, clung to his father. He could see in his father's face a struggle to comprehend the indescribable things enveloping them.

Then. . .the angel smiled at them and raised his hand in greeting! "Do not be afraid." His voice was deep yet warm. "I bring you good news of great joy that will be for all people. Today in the town of David a Savior has been born to you. He is the Messiah, the Lord. This will be a sign to you: You will find a baby wrapped in strips of cloth and lying in a manger."

The angels began to glow until the sky was brighter than noonday. With the increasing glow, they began to sing! The mighty army became a majestic choir. They filled the night with praises to Almighty God. . .They sang until the music filled the hearts of the shepherds, filling them with wonder, awe, and joy so incredible that they would be forever after at a loss to describe it to others. This was the music of the choir who sang to the King of the Universe. . .until now only heard in Heaven! The light of the angels glowed and changed with the melody of the music. . .the joy of God the Father poured out to a father and his son, and their shepherd friends.

Finally, the music finished and as quickly as they had appeared, the angels were gone. The night was there again, but somehow not nearly as dark. Together, the shepherds headed for Bethlehem, moving so fast that at times Isaac had to pick up his son Judah and carry him.

After a search through the village swollen with pilgrims, they were directed to a stable outside an inn that had no more vacancies. There, in hushed awe they found a man, his wife, and a newborn Baby wrapped in strips of cloth, His first bed the rough manger from which the animals ate. As they told the story of their incredible angelic visit, the mother and father nodded in understanding, their eyes bright.

Slowly Judah approached the manger, his father behind him with both hands resting gently on his shoulders. There, Judah and his father knelt down in front of the manger, the other shepherds crowded in close to see as well.

Judah's eyes were big and his mouth formed a small "ah" of awed amazement. The Baby looked up at him and for a brief moment their eyes met. This Baby. . .so small. . .so vulnerable. . .

so innocent. He reached out and touched the Baby's hand. Little fingers wrapped around his finger in an act of trust. Looking over at the Baby's mother and father, Judah asked, "What is His name?"

Joseph, the Baby's father, smiled back at Judah. "His name," he said, "is Jesus."

"Jesus." The name meant "Savior." Judah turned to look at his father and saw unashamed tears running down his face. "My son," Isaac whispered to him, "behold. . .the Lamb of God."

Judah nodded slowly. For a brief instant he thought of his Mitzar, and then he could see only the face of Jesus looking up at him from the manger. Never again would Judah look at a lamb the same way. . .nor would he look at God the same way. . . .

"Why, Father? Why is that man dying?" The voice of his son brought Judah back to the present. Here, on this spring day on a skull-shaped hill called Golgatha, he would share with his own son the truths his father had given him. It was time his son knew the truth. . .the Man on the middle Cross was the fulfillment of all Judah's father had taught him.

With tears streaming down his face, he knelt down next to his son and whispered, "My son. . . behold, the Lamb of God."

Some Words from the Artist

It's Never Too Late—Zechariah (Luke 1:5-80)

Eight days after John's birth he is circumcised according to Mosaic law in the home of Zechariah and Elizabeth or their synagogue. By tradition he now receives his name. Mute Zechariah holds up a wax-covered tablet inscribed in Hebrew (from right to left) *Yochanan smemo:* "John his name." *Yochanan* means "God's gracious gift" or "God is gracious."

Zechariah is depicted in authentic Jewish dress. He wears the white *kittel,* white symbolizing purity, simplicity, and humility. A white garment was worn every *Shabbat* (Sabbath) and on such solemn occasions as circumcisions. Around his waist is a braided belt, its intertwined strands of blue and white symbolic of good and evil intertwined in the heart (Jer. 17:9; Romans 7).

Draped over the *kittel* is a *tallit,* a rectangular woven piece of fabric. The tallit was the usual outer garment for Jewish men. The modern prayer shawl is still called a *tallit* or *tallis.* Zechariah's tallit would be hand woven and dyed of wool yarn, striped with the blue, purple, and scarlet of the temple.

The wooden tablet was covered with wax and etched with the wooden stylus. Then it was melted smooth in the sun. The flattened end of the stylus was for erasing. The writing is authentic in its grammar and calligraphy.

The architecture is intended to be symbolic. The wall's bricks and mortar call to mind that Israel slaves made bricks in Egypt. The sixty-six visible bricks (whole or in part) symbolize the thirty-nine Old Testament and twenty-seven New Testament books, God's complete revelation.

A wooden cross divides the left window. Knots in the wood are where the hands and feet of Messiah would be nailed to the Cross.

Made for a Miracle—Mary (Luke 1:26-56; 2:1-40)

She is a simple Jewish girl in her mid-teens. In a moment her reverie will be interrupted by an angel, whose emanating light falls on her back. Mary is dressed in white, symbolizing her virgin purity and humility. Her bare feet suggest the holiness of the moment (Exod. 3:5).

Like all winged creatures, the butterfly represents the spirit. The moth and butterfly are attracted to the light and so to the visible manifestation of the angel. This flight follows the path of

Mary's own submission to the light of revelation.

The crescent new moon symbolizes new beginnings of birth and marriage. The stars point to the faithfulness of God in keeping His covenants.

The tiny house in the right background is the house built by Joseph in the next story. To the right of the house is a cypress, and to the left of the house is a cedar. Trees connect heaven and earth; their roots penetrate the ground and their branches reach to the sky. Trees symbolize life, immortality, strength, and majesty. It was customary to plant a tree at the birth of a child—pine or cypress for a girl, cedar for a boy. Branches would be cut from these trees for their wedding canopy (*chuppah*).

Our Dream, His Time—Elizabeth (Luke 1)

At the sound of Mary's greeting, the unborn John leaps for joy in Elizabeth's womb, already herald of the Messiah.

The hanging drapery and darkened room from which she emerges, as well as her shadowed face, suggest the seclusion in which Elizabeth lived early in her pregnancy. Now, in her sixth month, when Mary visits, she comes forth into the light, literally and spiritually.

The blue and white of Elizabeth's head covering, robe, and skirt, as well as that of the drapery, refer to the heavenly care surrounding her special baby. The red drapery on Elizabeth's left, nailed to the door frame, alludes both to the Cross and to John's martyr death (Matt. 14:10). The purple border and gold embroidery of the drapery suggest the Messiah's kingship. The embroidery is of two alternating symbols of Israel. The seven-branched candlestand is the most ancient and enduring symbol of Israel kept in the tabernacle (Exod. 25:31-39) and temple (1 Kings 7:49). The Star of David implies the Davidic covenant and the humanity of the Messiah as the "Son of Man" (see, for example, Matt. 8:20; Mark 8:38; John 12:34).

Wedding rings did not become customary until the Middle Ages, but they were sometimes worn in late Bible times. The ring was placed by the groom on the index finger of his bride's right hand, as seen here. Beyond the meanings of the circle, the wedding ring represents unbreakable vows of mutual responsibility, protection, and faithfulness.

The Man God Trusted to Raise His Son—Joseph (Matt. 1:1-22:23)

Joseph wrestles with the fact of Mary's pregnancy. His carpenter's shop would have looked much like this. In the left foreground an unlit candle suggests Joseph's walk of faith, not sight (2 Cor. 5:7).

The mallet and three nails on the worktable allude to the Crucifixion, as do the crossed beams on the floor, the red band around Joseph's head (Christ's crown of thorns), his red skirt, and what appears to be a nail in his foot but actually is the screw of a C-clamp hanging on the wall. Knots in the beams are located where the hands and feet of the Messiah would be nailed to the Cross. Joseph's bare feet suggest the holiness of God's revelation to him in a dream.

The broken splintered boards describe Joseph's heart upon learning Mary is pregnant. The stone in the corner of the right foreground symbolizes Christ as "the chief cornerstone, the stone which the builders rejected" (Ps. 118:22; Matt. 21:42; Eph. 2:20).

On the shelf behind Joseph, the "A" formed by the compass and the "T" formed by the T-square are the first and last letters of the Hebrew alphabet, *aleph* and *taw* (read from right to left). They are like the Greek *alpha* and *omega,* "the first and the last" (Isa. 44:6; Rev. 1:8). The three linked S-hooks signify the Latin *Ter Sanctus:* "Holy, Holy, Holy."

The Price of a Room—The innkeeper (Luke 2:7)

The cross formed by the window panes alludes to the Crucifixion. Knots in the wood are located where the hands and feet of the Messiah would be nailed to the Cross. Here, the innkeeper is caught napping, suggesting that most people are asleep to the significance of the Cross as the primary reason the Messiah came.

Through Angels' Eyes—Michael and Gabriel (Luke 2:8-14)

There is no "right" way to view this picture, no top or bottom. It offers a slightly different perspective depending on how it stands. No direction is down in interstellar or interuniversal space. Nor is there gravity for beings who are pure spirit, if that is what angels are.

How large are these supernatural creatures? Perhaps some are gargantuan and others microscopic. Perhaps there is no such scale in their realm. Does spiritual light differ from visible wave lengths more than infrared differs from the light of a fluorescent tube? How clearly do angels' eyes see? Do they have gender?

To read what Scripture has to say about Gabriel, see Daniel 8:16-26; 9:21-27. To read about Michael, turn to Daniel 10:13-11:1; 12:1; Jude 9; Rev. 12:7-9.

The Gift of Joy—The shepherd brothers (Luke 2:8-20)

These hills accurately silhouette those near one of the shepherd fields by Bethlehem. The shepherds would have worn such varied, raggedy clothes. Behind the shepherd with a staff walks one holding the rod, a club referred to in Psalm 23:4. Both are sources of correction, comfort, and protection.

The sheep are a long-eared breed common in Israel. One appears to be wandering off (Ps. 119:176; Isa. 53:6; Matt. 18:12-13). The horned ram alludes to God's provision of a ram for Abraham, in place of Isaac (Gen. 22:13). The ram was used for many sacrifices. The *shofar,* a ram's horn trumpet, was blown to signal festivals and solemn assemblies.

The full moon suggests "the fullness of time." The stars are those seen in the winter, looking south toward Bethlehem.

The Star—The magi (Matt. 2:1-12)

The magi probably were astrologers from Media-Persia (now southern Iraq).

Leaving behind the dark tower of E-temananki, depicted here with the eight tiers described by the Greek historian Herodotus in the fifth century B.C., they follow west.

The star's seven-sided geometric form, which never appears in nature, seems a symbolic way to represent the invisible God. Its basic symmetry of seven beams, each of three circles (or spheres) of light, suggests the perfection of the triune God. Together, twenty-two points of light comprise the star, the number of letters in the Hebrew alphabet, connoting language, revelation, and the Word (John 1:1-14; 1 John 1:1-3).

The three-tiered crown worn by the magi originated in Babylon and was later worn by the Persian Zoroastrians. Its three tiers allude to the Trinity, while the three red rubies and six green emeralds signify the fruit of the Spirit (Gal. 5:22-23).

How many magi came? We only know it was more than one, because *magi* is plural. I depict seven (one only implied by shadow), symbolizing the perfection of God's plan of salvation. The three pack camels allude to the magi's gifts: Gold, frankincense, and myrrh. The donkey at the rear alludes to the humility of the Messiah (Zech. 9:9; Luke 19:29-44).

The full moon connects this picture in time and symbolism to the other pictures representing the birth night. The stars are also some seen in the southeast winter sky in Babylon.

The Distance of Faith—The religious leaders (Matt. 2:3-6)

The priest clutches a Torah scroll and holds a phylactery, a small, cube-shaped leather box containing Scriptural passages. It was traditionally worn on the left arm and forehead by men during prayers. On the phylactery is embossed the Hebrew letter *shin,* standing for *Shaddai* ("Almighty").

Torah (the books of Moses) was copied on lengths of parchment stitched together and wrapped around staves called "trees of life." When not read, a scroll was covered with a linen mantle. The red one here symbolizes the blood of the law.

The word *Torah* in Hebrew is embroidered in gold on the mantle. The embroidery also includes grapevines. Grapes were among the first fruits brought from Canaan (Numbers 13). Grapes connote fertility, life, peace, rebirth, and redemption (Ps. 80:9, 15; Jeremiah 2:21; 6:9; Hosea 10:1). Grapes ferment into wine, a dual symbol for blessing and curse. Wine means joy, celebration, thanksgiving, and gracious blessing, but also sacrifice. Passover celebrants drink from four cups of wine, symbolic of the paschal lamb's blood. At the Last Supper, Jesus used the third Passover cup, "the cup of redemption," to institute the Lord's Supper (Matt. 26:28).

Like wine, clouds have a dual association. They bring needed gentle rain, but also destructive storms and darkness. These clouds forebode Israel's destruction by Rome in A.D. 66-71. Yet, sunset also begins the Jewish day. A new day is coming in Messiah.

In the picture, a flock of forty ravens descends upon one dove, suggestive of the eventual opposition of Israel's leaders to Jesus, and to the forty years from Jesus' crucifixion in about the year A.D. 30 to the destruction of Jerusalem in A.D. 70.

In many cultures the dove symbolizes purity, chastity, innocence, and vulnerability. While the Temple stood, doves were brought as sacrificial offerings (Levit. 5:7; Luke 2:22-24). The song of the turtledove, a plaintive "cooing," is a harbinger of spring (Song 2:12) and means hope and rebirth. The raven is seen as ominous and cunning, unable to sing more than a harsh croak. While the dove was "clean" in the Mosaic dietary laws, the raven was "unclean" (Levit. 11:15). Nevertheless, the raven is the object of God's care (Job 38:41; Ps. 147:9). Ravens brought food to the prophet Elijah (1 Kings 17:2-6).

The architecture, bright white and apparently indestructible in the last rays of the setting sun, also alludes to the coming destruction. Herod began rebuilding the temple compound in 27 B.C., and it was completed only to be destroyed a few years later. Cracks in the wall behind the men suggest the crumbling facade of Jewish authority and the coming dispersion.

The Quiet Ones—Simeon and Anna (Luke 2:21-38)

Golden yellow light with seven beams of white depicts divine illumination and prophetic inspiration, the beams referring to the seven spirits of God (Isa. 11:2; Rev. 4:5).

The free-standing twin pillars of burnished copper refer back to those erected by King Solomon for the first temple (1 Kings 7:21; 2 Chron. 3:17; Ezek. 40:49), though not duplicated by Herod.

Simeon wears a prayer shawl, typically white with black stripes. While Luke tells us Simeon held Jesus in his arms, I cannot imagine that Anna did not also, once her eyes beheld the Hope of her long life. The forty-day-old baby, the incarnate Word of God, touches her lips, enabling her to "speak of Him to all those who were looking for the redemption of Jerusalem."

Threat to the Throne—Herod (Matt. 2:1-18)

The horror of the slaughter in Bethlehem reflects in the violent rage of the man who ordered it. Self-imposed nightmares such as this may have haunted Herod after he ordered the execution of his favorite wife and three of his sons. The four shrouded figures allude to them, and to hundreds of other people Herod had executed out of paranoia of losing his throne. This fear drove him to slaughter Bethlehem's infant boys.

The red carpet and drapery (reflected in the sword blade) recall the blood-soaked trail of Herod's life. The column and drapery form a "cross," pointing toward the eventual death of the Messiah—in God's time, not Herod's.

Christmas Lamb—Shepherd father and son (Luke 2:9-14; 23:35)

These shepherds are also dressed historically. The father's staff without the curved end was actually more common than the staff depicted on page 54. The red scarf "covering" the father and falling below the head and throat of the lamb signifies the sacrifice of the innocent lamb. The small mole on both the father's and son's right cheek suggests their genetic connection, and also the similar "imperfections" (sin) inherent in everyone.

The pink and blue light bathing the man and the boy connect this picture to the angels on page 48, specifically to Gabriel. Perhaps one of these angels had been the one who first bore the glad tidings to the shepherds.